The Art of Business Communication

PEARSON

At Pearson, we believe in learning – all kinds of learning for all kinds of people. Whether it's at home, in the classroom or in the workplace, learning is the key to improving our life chances.

That's why we're working with leading authors to bring you the latest thinking and best practices, so you can get better at the things that are important to you. You can learn on the page or on the move, and with content that's always crafted to help you understand quickly and apply what you've learned.

If you want to upgrade your personal skills or accelerate your career, become a more effective leader or more powerful communicator, discover new opportunities or simply find more inspiration, we can help you make progress in your work and life.

Pearson is the world's leading learning company. Our portfolio includes the Financial Times and our education business, Pearson International.

Every day our work helps learning flourish, and wherever learning flourishes, so do people.

To learn more, please visit us at **www.pearson.com/uk**

The Art of Business Communication

How to use pictures, charts and graphs to make your message stick

Graham Shaw

PEARSON

Harlow, England • London • New York • Boston • San Francisco • Toronto • Sydney
Auckland • Singapore • Hong Kong • Tokyo • Seoul • Taipei • New Delhi
Cape Town • São Paulo • Mexico City • Madrid • Amsterdam • Munich • Paris • Milan

Pearson Education Limited
Edinburgh Gate
Harlow CM20 2JE
United Kingdom
Tel: +44 (0)1279 623623
Web: www.pearson.com/uk

First edition published 2015 (print and electronic)

© Pearson Education Limited 2015 (print and electronic)

The right of Graham Shaw to be identified as author of this work has been asserted by him in accordance with the Copyright, Designs and Patents Act 1988.

Pearson Education is not responsible for the content of third-party internet sites.

ISBN: 978–1-292–01717–4 (print)
       978–1-292–01719–8 (PDF)
       978–1-292–01720–4 (ePub)
       978–1-292–01718–1 (eText)

British Library Cataloguing-in-Publication Data
A catalogue record for the print edition is available from the British Library

Library of Congress Cataloging-in-Publication Data
Shaw, Graham.
  The art of business communication : how to use pictures, charts and graphs to make your message stick / Graham Shaw.
     pages cm
  Includes bibliographical references and index.
  ISBN 978-1-292-01717-4 (print : alk. paper) -- ISBN 978-1-292-01719-8 (PDF) --
ISBN 978-1-292-01720-4 (ePub) -- ISBN 978-1-292-01718-1 (eText)
  1. Business communication. 2. Visual communication. 3. Visual aids. I. Title.
  HF5718.S464 2015
  658.4'5--dc23
                          2014035176

10 9 8 7 6 5 4 3 2 1
18 17 16 15 14

Cover design by redeyoffdesign.com

Print edition typeset in 10.25 pt Frutiger LT Pro by 3
Printed in Great Britain by Henry Ling Ltd, at the Dorset Press, Dorchester, Dorset

NOTE THAT ANY PAGE CROSS REFERENCES REFER TO THE PRINT EDITION

Contents

About the author

Graham Shaw is Managing Director of Vision Learning and Development and specialises in the art of communication. As a conference speaker and trainer he has worked with numerous major organisations worldwide. He is best known for his use of fast drawings to bring ideas to life and make messages stick. Thousands of people have benefited from his workshops on professional presenting and visual communication. In addition to his corporate work, Graham takes his skills into schools to help children and students apply visual techniques to boost their learning ability.

To learn more about Graham's work visit www.visionlearning.co.uk

Acknowledgements

I would like to thank everyone who has influenced my thinking and development and thereby made it possible for me to write this book.

Firstly, I owe huge thanks to the team at Pearson for their excellent support. A special thank you goes to Eloise Cook, my superb commissioning editor, for her perceptive feedback and great encouragement throughout. She saw the potential for this book and without her it would never have happened. I am also very appreciative of Melanie Carter, project editor, for all her brilliant work and also thankful to Lucy Carter for her very positive support.

I am most grateful to those who have helped me develop my ideas over the years through mentoring, coaching or simply giving their time. In this respect I am particularly appreciative of the generous support of: Bernard Amos, Patrick and Kimberley Hare, Nigel and Jenny Heath, Jan Jewers, Chris McCloskey and Louise Robb.

Thanks to my teachers in the field of Neuro-Linguistic Programming (NLP). In particular I have learnt so much from Sue Knight, John Overdurf, Julie Silverthorn and Ian Ross. I also thank all the other numerous trainers with whom I have worked and who have been so generous in sharing ideas. Likewise thanks to the many clients and workshop participants, including school teachers, students and children. They have all played a part in helping me to shape my ideas and therefore influenced my work.

A special thank you to my fantastic assistant, Ann McCullough, not only for checking of the manuscript, but for all her years of excellent support for my professional work.

I especially thank Lynda, my wife, for her total support and patience as I spent numerous hours working on the book, and for her considerable help in testing ideas and checking drafts.

To my sons David and Andrew who, in following their passion, inspire me to follow mine. Thank you both. Let your lights shine in the world.

Finally, thank you to my wonderful parents – my mother Mary and my late father, Bill. He is still my inspiration.

I dedicate this book to Bill and Mary Shaw.

Introduction: Why visual works

This book is all about drawing simple sketches to help you and others to communicate business ideas. The skills can be applied easily in many work situations including team meetings, one-to-one communication and presentations, training or coaching. You may not yet believe that you can draw. However by the word 'draw' I'm not talking about being able to produce masterpieces like Leonardo da Vinci. Rather I am referring to the ability to be able to draw perfectly acceptable sketches to a standard that is good enough to get an idea across to others.

Something magical happens when you draw your idea 'live'

As well as learning to create pre-prepared drawings, you will learn the skills of drawing a 'live' picture to explain an idea. By this I mean drawing 'on-the-fly' so that you sketch an idea as you explain it. There is a world of difference between simply presenting pre-prepared images and drawing 'live' as you speak. The moment you move your pen on the paper those watching are hooked. They are transfixed as their eyes follow your every stroke and you have them captivated. Furthermore, by using this technique people can absorb the information so easily and recall it later just as if they were still watching you.

This method of communicating is dramatic and so effective yet vastly underused.

You will learn to draw 'live' to capture attention – but you may not believe it yet

With the help of my character Spike, above, I will help you to learn to draw your own pictures to explain ideas in memorable ways whether in one-to-one or group settings.

In proposing the use of sketches I am not ruling out showing pictures electronically. Both methods have their advantages. Rather, I am suggesting that the use of drawing skills is a valuable addition, and at times a brilliant alternative, to traditional electronic methods.

In my work as a speaker and trainer I have used drawing for many years to communicate ideas and information. I have often heard people say they wished they could draw to explain ideas in business meetings and presentations. This really motivated me to develop ways of helping people to be able to draw for themselves.

If you are interested in learning any of the following then this book is for you.

How can you:

- grab the attention of people with a quick sketch?
- make your ideas memorable?
- keep people engaged?
- encourage teams to work collaboratively?
- explain ideas easily and quickly?
- get ideas across visually when coaching or training others?
- differentiate yourself as a speaker?

By understanding how to apply some simple drawing skills and link them to speaking skills you will be able to transform your ability to engage individuals and groups.

No drawing experience required

If you already have some drawing experience then great, if not that's fine too.

All you need to be successful is to:

- **just have a go** – it's amazing what you can learn when you just give it a go; and
- **keep an open mind** – rather like a parachute, the mind works best when it is open. When you keep your mind open you are receptive to learning and develop faster.

You already have the ability to draw but you may not have discovered it yet

If you do not believe you have the ability to draw, just have a go at the exercise below.

We are going to draw my character, Spike. All you have to do is to pick up your pen and draw along with me.

Just follow my lines and instructions:

So we start with the nose.

Now the eyes, like 66 or speech marks.

Now a nice big smile.

Next the ear and a little line for detail inside.

Now his hair sticking up.

Next a line for the left side of the face.

Then place the pen just under the ear and drop a line down for the back of the neck.

Now the collar of his T-shirt.

Then a line to the left for his shoulder.

And a line to the right for his other shoulder.

If you have drawn Spike you can draw everything else in this book

If you can draw Spike you have all the ability you need to draw simple pictures to communicate with people in engaging and memorable ways.

What are the key benefits of pictures?

A picture is worth a thousand words

Words can often be inefficient at expressing ideas compared with the power of pictures as the following figure illustrates.

Description	Image
A curved line with every point equidistant from the centre	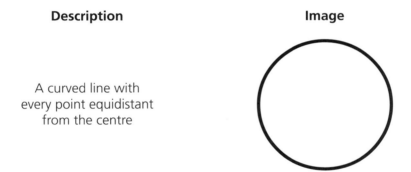

In *The Mind Map Book*, Tony Buzan gives an insight into why pictures are so powerful:

> *'The reason why, to quote the old adage, pictures are "worth a thousand words" is that they make use of a massive range of cortical skills: colour, form, line, dimension, texture, visual rhythm, and especially imagination.'*

The whole point of this book is to build your skill of turning words and thoughts into pictures.

Pictures can be very memorable

The amazing power of pictures to stay in the memory is well documented. Buzan refers to the following examples of impressive research by Ralph Haber and Raymond Nickerson.

In 1970 the journal *Scientific American* reported on the work of Ralph Haber. He devised experiments to test the ability of the brain to recognise pictures. In one such test he showed subjects 2560 slides, one every 10 seconds. Viewings were carried out in sessions over a few days' duration, but the total time spent actually viewing the slides was seven hours. One hour after the final viewing he tested the ability of people to remember the pictures. He showed them 2560 pairs of slides that comprised one slide from the original set that they had seen before along with one picture that was new to them. The subjects were asked to say which pictures they had seen before. They were able to do this with an average accuracy of between 85 and 95 per cent.

Furthermore he found that even if he only showed the slides for one second each it made no difference to the results. He was even able to reverse the pictures to show the mirror image with no adverse effect on the results. Haber concluded:

> *'These experiments with visual stimuli suggest that recognition of pictures is essentially perfect.'*

Some pictures are easier to remember than others

Even more impressive results were demonstrated by Raymond Nickerson and reported in the *Canadian Journal of Psychology*. He found that if pictures were really vivid then the ability of people to recall them markedly increased. In an experiment using 10,000 *vivid* pictures Nickerson's subjects were able to say with 99.9 per cent accuracy whether they had seen a particular picture before.

When pictures are unusual they are easier to recall

When we think of this in relation to using pictures to explain ideas, we can see that by paying attention to the types of pictures we use we can make a big difference to the ability of people to recall them. When we make pictures colourful, different, imaginative or unusual they are much more likely to be easily absorbed and easier to recall than dull or ordinary images.

The ability for the brain to remember pictures is almost limitless

Linking a picture with an idea helps us remember it

The brain's natural ability to make imaginative links is a key factor in helping us to remember. We all have experiences of associating one thing with another. A piece of music may bring back memories of an experience such as a holiday.

This means that learning to draw will help us to make imaginative links that will make our ideas easier to absorb and recall. Therefore, by drawing a picture to go with a word or phrase we can make it more memorable.

Use both a word and a picture to make your idea memorable

Showing a picture whilst speaking works well for the listener

People find it really easy to look at a picture whilst listening to a voice. One only has to think of young children looking at pictures whilst the story is being told. When news is broadcast on television the power of the pictures is a perfect complement to the voice of the newsreader. In communicating your ideas you can create the same effect when you use suitable pictures and interact with them in an appropriate way.

However, in presentations many people tend to be reading or summarising the text in a presentation whilst the audience is reading it simultaneously. This practice has been shown to be fraught with problems and is one of the key reasons why people find it so difficult and often tedious to sit through a series of electronic slides.

People cannot read text and listen effectively at the same time

The fact is that the brain is just not wired to read and listen at the same time. Research from the University of New South Wales concluded that people process information perfectly well in verbal or written form, but not in both at the same time. Therefore it is not helpful to present a lot of text on a presentation slide and expect people to read it while you speak.

The brain cannot effectively read and listen at the same time

People find it really hard to keep concentration levels up when faced with lots of text in a presentation. If you have very brief amounts of text, for example just one line or a few bullet points, then people can cope better with listening. However, even then, to repeatedly be talking while showing text is going to become wearing for the listener. Therefore use pictures wherever possible.

Pictures look different – words look very similar

Sometimes people feel that when giving a presentation the key thing is to have all of their points written for the audience to see. This practice tends to lead to a set of slides being produced that are, largely, written bullet points. The problem with this is that lines of text look rather similar.

Lines of text look rather similar

Whether printed on a screen, written on a whiteboard or flipchart paper, the overall perception is that each slide or page looks very much like the previous one. One of the key problems with this, in terms of memory, is that we know that the brain recalls things that are different more easily than many items that are similar. The brain enjoys variation and this is another reason why the repetitious format of text is unhelpful.

Drawings do not have to be brilliant – it is not what makes them memorable

The great news is that to make drawings memorable does not require that the drawings themselves are of a brilliant standard. In fact very simple and basic drawings can work better. There are so many important factors that make a picture easy to recall and the standard of drawing is definitely not one of them. The brain is picking up on so many other visual cues other than the drawing quality.

What if PowerPoint is expected?

As mentioned earlier, I am suggesting drawing skills as an additional tool that may be used alongside methods such as PowerPoint. A presentation could involve many different methods of getting ideas across (e.g. drawings, PowerPoint, videos or demonstrations).

On the specific question of PowerPoint being expected, I would say that, in my experience, the listeners usually are more concerned with whether the speaker is interesting or not than they are with the methods used. Regardless of the techniques you use, if you are keeping people engaged, I would be surprised if someone complains that they wished you had used PowerPoint.

So how will we go about learning?

- First we will build our drawing skills, enabling you to draw lots of useful pictures and symbols.
- Next we will learn how to think in pictures so that we can represent ideas visually.
- Then we will explore how to use many different methods to apply our drawing skills when explaining ideas to individuals or groups.
- I will also highlight ways to assist teams to use sketches to share ideas and how to collaborate more effectively will also be highlighted.
- Finally you will find I have created a Visual Toolkit for you. This last chapter provides a range of simple symbols that you can use time and again to illustrate many different concepts.

Just get drawing – and realise how quickly you can learn

I have worked with many people who thought they could not draw. Through practice and repetition of my simple steps they found that they are capable of producing very acceptable sketches that are easily good enough to communicate ideas.

How to get the best from this book

This is a practical book and the aim is to get the skills into the muscle. I want you to actually acquire drawing skills that you can demonstrate.

Therefore you will find it helpful to:

- Have a pen and paper to hand so you can sketch as you read the book.
- Feel free to draw any pictures that capture your interest.
- Repeat the drawing skills in odd moments to make them automatic.
- Realise that mistakes with drawings is normal – in fact these are a helpful part of learning.
- Enjoy learning – this is the most important thing.

By the end of the book you will have started on a journey of developing skills that you can use immediately to enhance your communication skills.

The key thing is to start putting your skills into practice straight away. You will be amazed at the positive reaction of people when they see you are using drawing skills that they do not imagine they could achieve themselves. Furthermore, as you engage them fully you will find that people absorb your ideas effortlessly and can recall them easily. What more could they want?

We will now move on to start learning our drawing skills

So grab yourself a pencil and paper and be ready to embark on the journey of learning how to draw in order to communicate ideas.

Spike will help you learn to draw and present your ideas.

Just follow along and enjoy learning!

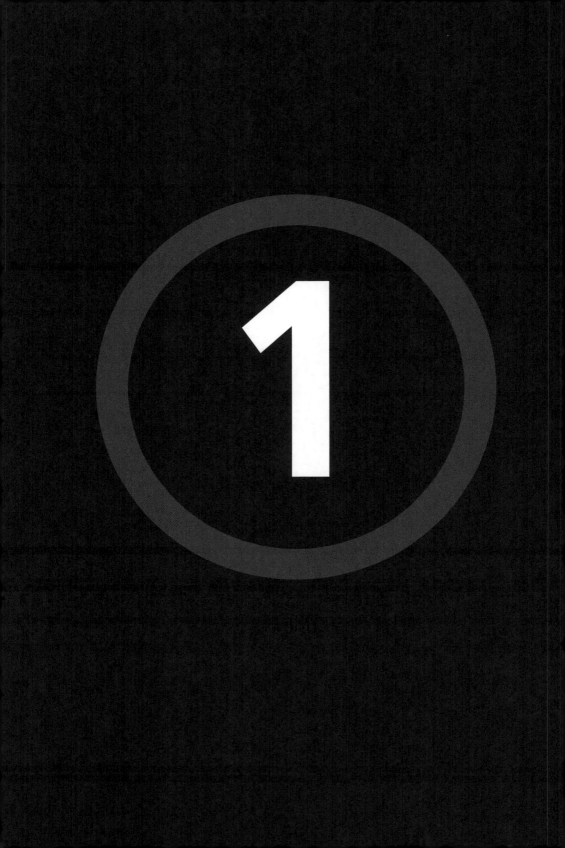

Building your drawing skills

To explain ideas in pictures we just need to be able to draw images that represent physical things and abstract concepts. In order to do this we need to write or draw the following:

- words;
- people;
- shapes;
- symbols.

A few simple lines make it easy to draw

It is a myth that in order to recognise a picture all the details need to be present, in fact the reverse is often true. Paradoxically, often less is more. You would be amazed at how little you need to draw in order to create a recognisable image. This is because of the brain's astonishing ability to make meaning. In terms of perception the brain is very good at interpreting very limited visual information and making sense of it. This is why just a few lines will do the trick.

Therefore there is a huge benefit in economy of line when drawing. The fewer lines you have, the easier it is for you to draw. It is actually quite possible to draw recognisable pictures with just a few strokes.

This means that, even with no previous experience, you can soon be drawing great pictures. When you find a sketch easy to do, you can quickly make it automatic by repeating it just a few times.

So let's get drawing

This is a practical section in which we look at how to build up your ability to draw and think in pictures.

People – faces and expressions to depict emotions

We sketched our character Spike earlier on and you may well remember the sequence in which we drew him. In this case we are going to use him as an example of how easy it is to draw a range of different expressions conveying different emotions.

Have a go
First have a go at drawing Spike again and see if you can remember the sequence of lines.

Draw Spike several times to get the learning into the muscle.

You might notice the lines do not always turn out exactly the same and that is just fine. We are not aiming for perfection, we are simply trying to sketch an image that is good enough to convey an idea. It is natural not to get everything exactly perfect to start with and, with practice, you will become more consistent.

You have already learnt how to draw thousands of characters

Yes, you might want to read that again because actually. . .

The secret is in the sequence

Whilst you may think that you have learned to draw just Spike, the fact is that you have learnt a strategy that will enable you to draw endless different characters with all kinds of expressions and emotions.

It really is that simple

The same sequence you learned for drawing Spike can be used to draw lots of other expressions and also different characters.

Stick to the sequence – but just make slight variations to your lines

All you need to do is use the same sequence but then make variations to your lines, for example a downward line for the mouth would make him look unhappy. Drawing different hair would create a different character altogether.

Let's start experimenting with some variations for spike

First we will give Spike some different expressions.

Use the same sequence of lines again but this time notice that we are changing the expression.

Have a go

Just draw a downward mouth to make Spike look unhappy.

Just a circle shaded in for the mouth for a shocked expression.

Just a dot for the mouth makes him look puzzled.

The same sequence can be used to create lots of other characters with different emotions. We will draw some examples later.

Now let us see how easy it is to draw action.

Simple figures to depict action

Here we look at drawing stick figures. When we want to draw people, stick figures work just as well as trying to draw more complex full figures. Remember that when we are drawing for communicating it is not about the finished result. Rather it is about drawing pictures that can be recognised and easily recalled. The brain will find it just as easy to remember a stick figure as it will a much more realistic representation of a person. Furthermore, stick figures are an excellent way to show action and any sort of movement.

Have a go

Just draw the figures below and create some variations of your own.

Standing   Walking   Running   Jumping

Stick figures in different situations

Now let us see how easy it is to put our stick figures into different situations.

Have a go

Just sketch the pictures below.

| Sitting | Working at a desk |

Our simple stick figures are really useful for all kinds of pictures.

Symbols and simple pictures

We will now learn how to draw simple pictures that are good enough to convey the idea we want to get across to others. Remember this is not about being able to do fantastic drawings. We just need to be able to draw images that will help us to explain ideas.

You can create thousands of pictures from basic shapes

In this exercise you will get used to building up pictures.

Have a go

All you have to do is look at the shapes below and draw them on your piece of paper. Then what I would like you to do is to look at each shape in turn and think about what it could be. By adding more lines or shapes, you can turn it into something that we would recognise. I have drawn examples below. Have a go at those and see if you can draw something different.

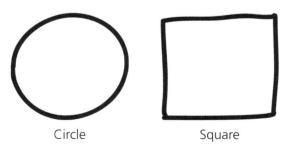

| Circle | Square |

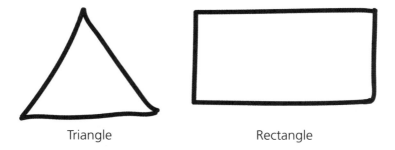

Triangle   Rectangle

These simple shapes can be transformed.

Clock   House

Yacht   Lorry

How did you get on? Inevitably some drawings will be better than others. The key thing is to be able to make recognisable pictures.

To draw something – just think of the first shape you need

Some pictures are composed of a number of simple shapes put together. When we think of drawing in this way it makes it much easier to attempt to draw a picture that previously we may not have tried.

Have a go

Copy my drawings below. Just start with a basic shape and then add in the details.

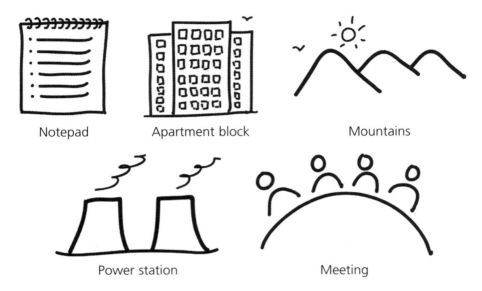

| Notepad | Apartment block | Mountains |

| Power station | Meeting |

Now let's draw different characters

In this exercise we learn how easy it is to draw a range of different characters and thereby immediately expand your drawing repertoire.

Notice how we can build up the drawing with lines in the same sequence as when we drew Spike. Then we just begin to create some variations to make totally new characters.

Have a go

Just draw the characters below. Then have a go at creating other characters of your own.

The main lines are the same as for Spike – just different hair and we have a new character

Use the same sequence again – just altering nose and hair

Here we draw an open mouth – just a triangle

Change the hair for a different character – now we try round eyes too

This character looks in the other direction

For glasses, just draw the frames and put dots in for the eyes

Now let's see how easy it is to draw characters from the front

Drawing from the front is really simple. In fact pictures such as these are often good enough to use rather than adding other features such as hair and clothes.

The pictures below are quick and easy to draw so really useful to have up your sleeve when using pictures to communicate ideas.

Have a go

Just try these and see how easy they are.

Happy, contented, satisfied, pleased: just draw a circle first

Unhappy, gloomy, disappointed, dejected: just a curve down for the mouth

Puzzled, thoughtful, wondering, curious: even just a dot creates an expression

Cheerful, laughing, happy: get used to drawing open mouths

One drawing can depict many emotions

Lines and shapes that communicate ideas

It is not all about pictures. By using simple lines and shapes we can communicate ideas really well. All you need is to be able to draw a range such as those below. You can create all kinds of models and diagrams with your lines and shapes. You can combine them with the pictures and symbols to get your ideas across in imaginative and engaging ways. They can just be drawn freehand and fairly quickly.

Have a go

Draw the examples below and create some variations of your own.

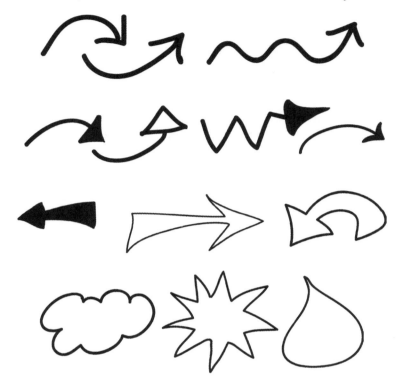

Putting it all together

See below how easy it is to combine our basic shapes and lines to create pictures to express ideas. Even a quickly drawn sketch can convey lots of useful information in an easy-to-understand way.

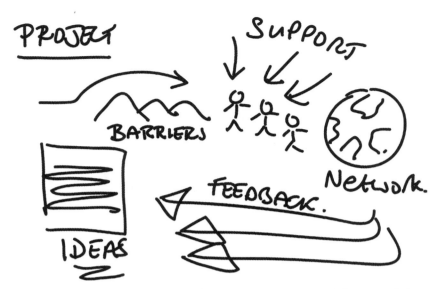

People can literally see what you mean with a quick sketch

Teams can sketch ideas together to express their thoughts

Keep practising – you will be amazed how quickly your skills develop

Even doodling when you have an idle few minutes can help to build up your drawing ability. You will be amazed how quickly many of the drawings become automatic for you. It only takes several practices for you to get the skills into the 'muscle'.

Summary

- Keep your drawings simple – they are then easier and more memorable.

- All objects are composed of basic shapes – so just start with a shape.

- Adapt Spike to create other characters.

- Draw faces from the front by drawing a circle or oval.

- Draw stick figures to show action.

- Get used to drawing various arrows, shapes and lines.

- Add simple details to create variety in your repertoire of shapes and symbols.

More practice

To reinforce and develop your drawing skills, have a go at the following. See if you are able to do each one without looking at previous pictures. If you do need help, though, you can always check back – that is what the pictures are there for.

- Draw four different happy faces: two male two female.
- Draw the characters again: but this time give each person one of the following expressions, so that they each show a different emotion:
  - sad;
  - shocked;
  - unhappy;
  - thoughtful.
- Draw a stick figure doing the following:
  - standing upright hands on hips;
  - standing upright arms in the air;
  - running;
  - walking;
  - jumping over a wall;
  - kicking a ball.
- Do a quick sketch to show
  - two people climbing a mountain;
  - a van travelling at speed;
  - person seated at a desk;
  - four people at a meeting table;
  - person running through a forest;
  - person on a diving board;
  - ship at sea with the sun shining.
- Experiment with drawing: choose whatever you would like to practise. Have a go at some drawings that you find easy and also choose some that you find more challenging.

How to think in pictures

Now we have built up our skill in drawing simple symbols and pictures we will move on to look at pictures and meaning. The purpose of this is to help us when communicating ideas and information.

Attaching meaning to pictures

Pictures can mean many things. This is good news for us because it means that every picture we can draw may be used to convey numerous ideas. Here you will see a number of pictures with potential meanings.

As you look at them, see what other meanings come into your mind.

Achievement; victory; goal

Solid; ecological; environment

We are all on board; we are in this together; we are all at sea

Trust; teamwork; balance

One symbol can mean many things

This may seem a rather obvious learning point, however it is fundamental to assisting us in being able to easily represent many different ideas. There could be numerous other interpretations of these pictures. I could have written many other meanings, so there are no right or wrong answers.

The important point is this, however, if one symbol can have multiple meanings this means that. . .

We can use the same symbols over and over again

This means we can get a lot of use from each picture we can draw. One reason why we can use one symbol for many different meanings is that, once we suggest a meaning for a symbol, the brain will easily accept this, providing it is plausible enough. This is all to do with the role of suggestion in guiding our perception. When we take in information we are always seeking meaning as we try to make sense of it.

When we receive a suggestion as to what something might mean we seek to fit our perception accordingly. You may have come across the example of a person walking through long grass and mistaking a piece of hose for a snake. Providing the suggested meaning makes sense, we are highly likely to accept it.

This is one of the reasons why I suggest using a word or phrase along with the picture. Whilst a picture may say 1000 words on its own, our word or phrase will ensure that the specific meaning we have in mind is exactly how the audience will interpret that picture.

Using words and pictures together makes a powerful link

When we use a word and picture together we can create a powerful link and it is by making such connections that we help ideas to stay in the memory. The more creative and unusual these links are, the more effective as far as memory is concerned.

Thinking of pictures for meanings

Have a go

Let us get used to thinking in pictures.

For each word below I have sketched three examples of pictures to represent it.

Have a go at sketching my examples.

Then see what other pictures come into your mind to represent each word and, finally, draw your own pictures.

Remember, it is not about every picture you come up with being brilliant. It is actually more important just to practise. Through trial and error soon you will start to improve your ability to think of pictures and be able to draw them.

Teamwork

Success

Results

Vision

Each word can be represented in many different pictures

There is no particular picture that represents a given idea. As long as your picture is a near enough approximation in terms of meaning, then you will be able to use it to communicate an idea.

How to make ideas easier to remember

The following applies both to pictures and the words attached to them.

Colourful

The brain loves colour so use it to help with recognition and recall of images. There are great benefits to including colour, and advantages when we use certain colours to represent particular ideas. This is because some colours already have natural associations for people. Sometimes the meanings of colours can be subjective, but often there is widespread agreement as to what certain colours represent.

The following examples illustrate this point:

- red = danger, alarm, hazardous, hot;
- yellow = positive, optimistic, bright, cheerful, sunny;
- green = natural, environmental, eco-friendly.

When an appropriate colour is used it serves to convey meaning more powerfully. It also makes the information easier to recall.

Difference and contrast

People find it easier to recall things that stand out or are very different from other things. When you want elements of a picture to be noticed, a simple way to achieve this is to make those elements very different from everything else. This could be a contrast in colour, size or some other attribute.

Exaggeration

One sure-fire way to make an idea stand out is through exaggeration.

In fact exaggeration combined with contrast is a really simple way to show a difference visually between two concepts. For example, you may be talking about contrasting concepts such as big/small, low/high, narrow/wide, inexpensive/costly, unprofitable/profitable, operational/strategic, less/more, up/down and so on. All of these concepts lend themselves to exaggeration and contrast visually, in order to make the point obvious.

The following two pictures show exaggeration to make one element stand out.

Write words in ways that illustrate their meaning

We can get quite creative not only with colours, but also in the imaginative ways we can write a word to emphasise its meaning.

Here are four examples.

Keep practising – and you will find it easy to think in pictures

Once you get used to thinking in pictures, you will find it gets easier to come up with ideas. The trick is just to start drawing and often you will find that the idea develops as you draw. It is rarely the case that the idea is fully formed in your head first. The act of drawing itself helpfully prompts the thought process.

Summary

- Use a word and picture together – to make a memorable link.

- One picture will represent many ideas – so use the same pictures many times.

- Make subtle variations to symbols and use them again in different ways.

- Draw just enough lines for people to see the picture.

- Just see what images pop into your mind when thinking of pictures.

- Use colour, contrast and exaggeration to make pictures easy to remember.

More practice

- Draw a symbol or picture to represent each of the following:
  - action;
  - energy;
  - environment;
  - idea;
  - global;
  - data;
  - knowledge;
  - flexibility;
  - harmony;
  - research.

Tip: If the first picture that comes into your mind seems too difficult to draw, think of a different image. There will always be an easier one.

Communicating with drawings

In this chapter we will look at how we can use our drawing skills for communicating ideas. You may want to encourage others to draw as well as using sketching skills yourself. Perhaps you need to explain ideas or explore issues in meetings, during presentations or even in one-to-one situations. These are all really useful everyday applications for your drawing skills.

How can drawings help us to communicate?

Whether you are creating the drawings yourself or assisting teams to do so, there are plenty of ways in which creating pictures can help communication in your business.

It's an immediate and informal way to express ideas

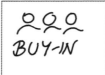

Sketching ideas is a refreshingly informal way to get thoughts across. Just pen and paper make it possible to use your drawing skills virtually anywhere and in almost any situation when you need to explain information or ideas.

Shared visual language enhances joint understanding

It can be difficult at a meeting for people to understand colleagues' ideas and information. Furthermore, it is impossible for them to see ideas in their minds in the same way as their colleagues. This leads to many different interpretations and misunderstandings.

As people collaborate to create pictures to express their ideas they develop a common visual language. This helps them increase their joint understanding of the topics and issues they are exploring. It can make it possible for people to literally 'see' a colleague's point of view or way of thinking.

Easy to see the big picture

Drawing is a great way for everyone to see the big picture. Whether this is a business process, model or diagram, people can see the whole idea in one image. This gives a focal point for discussion and makes it easier for people to contribute to the discussion.

Relationships between elements are easily seen

When an idea is explained verbally it is not always easy to see how the elements relate to each other. This is especially so if the idea is at all complex. Once ideas are expressed visually it becomes really easy to see the relationships between the component parts. This means people can also more easily see problems or new possibilities. Having the picture visible makes it easy for them to point out their observations to colleagues.

Visuals can be modified to show new connections

Once people have a picture such as a model or diagram to look at they will see immediately not only existing relationships but new connections between elements. Having the whole picture visible enables them to add, subtract or modify parts of the picture easily. In this way the visual is far from a static image, but instead becomes a dynamic tool that enables people to not only share ideas, but also to develop and modify their thinking.

Increased ownership by creating something tangible together

One of the biggest challenges in meetings is getting buy-in and ownership for ideas and decisions. One way to encourage ownership and buy-in is to have people involved in developing those ideas and making decisions. When people engage in creating something tangible together they are much more likely to own it and feel it is a part of themselves. Their level of commitment to its content is therefore much more likely to be high.

It's active and creates a positive energy

We know just how much state of mind affects performance, whatever the discipline. Whether it is music, sport or business, how someone feels directly affects their ability to work effectively. Drawing ideas as a team really does create an energetic and positive atmosphere. This in turn leads to people being alert yet relaxed which is a productive state.

Creativity and imagination are encouraged

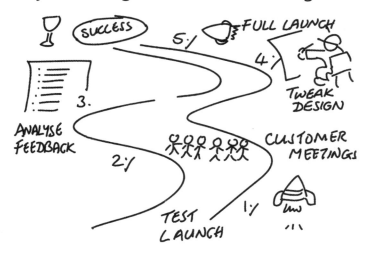

Drawing together helps to spark new ideas as people jointly contribute to the development of a picture. As people begin to add parts to the picture, this will prompt others to see ways to build further. An additional factor is that people associate drawing with creativity and therefore the very act of drawing is seen immediately as creative.

It builds the team

Drawing ideas together is a great team-working activity. People are working cooperatively and, even if not everyone is actually drawing on the board, they are all involved in its creation by contributing ideas. As they create the picture, model or diagram together they learn more about the strengths of team members and their contribution to the team.

Drawing choices

Pre-prepared drawings

This is where you draw everything in advance and then use your picture to help your explanation.

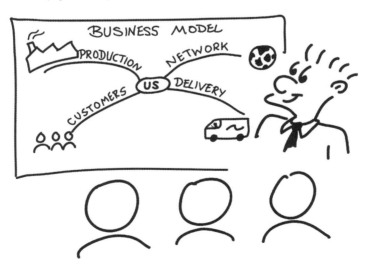

Spike has his drawing pre-prepared

Pros

- Useful way to start until you feel more confident drawing while you speak.
- You have time to ensure you draw a good standard picture.
- Can be easier for you to present than drawing 'live' – leaves you free to concentrate on speaking without being concerned with drawing at the same time.

Cons

- The least engaging approach as it lacks the effect of seeing the picture emerge.
- More similar to the way people expect presentations to be – therefore loss of opportunity to differentiate yourself in a dramatic way.

Partly-prepared drawings

This is where you draw part of the picture in advance and then draw the rest as you explain it.

The visual is prepared partly in advance – then the rest drawn 'live'

Pros

- Allows you to prepare the more tricky elements in advance.
- Gives you an easier step into 'live' drawing than starting from a totally blank sheet.
- Intrigue and curiosity can be created because people will wonder what is missing.
- Still leaves the chance for you to captivate them with elements of drawing 'on-the-fly'.

Cons

- Lacks the attention-hooking potential of the 'blank page' start.

Pre-prepared pictures placed one by one onto a board in sequence

In this variation you draw pictures in advance but then present them one at a time. You could sketch pictures onto sticky notes or cards first. Then make sure you have them ordered in a suitable sequence enabling you to stick them up on a surface one at a time to tell your story.

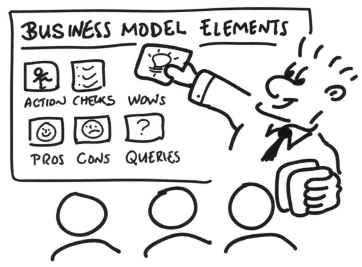

Spike's drawings are already done on coloured cards – he then builds the storyboard

This is also great for teams who can prepare a series of pictures (e.g. on coloured cards or sticky notes) and have them ready to place up on a board. It is an excellent way to tell a story or present a model.

Pros

- A great method for teams to record and present ideas to colleagues.
- If you are apprehensive about drawing 'live' this is a good alternative.
- Offers the best of both worlds, i.e. you can prepare in advance but, by introducing one picture at a time, you can get the effect of the whole visual building up.
- Can be quicker to present ideas than using 'live' sketching.
- Even complex visuals can be absorbed easily because they are built up gradually.

Cons

- Requires a lot more preparation than sketching 'live'.
- Does not have the same magical effect as 'live' drawing.

'On-the-fly' – 'live' drawing

This is where you start with a blank sheet and you draw whilst talking.

Spike starts with a blank sheet and builds the picture 'live'

Pros

- This method is attention-grabbing and engaging.
- A high degree of suspense and curiosity is possible right from the start.
- Even detailed visuals can be followed and remembered when they are built up gradually.
- You are in complete control – you can add lines at will, stop and start.
- It looks impressive and differentiates you as a speaker.

Cons

- You need to be well-practised if the visual is at all complex.
- May take longer to show a given amount of information compared to pre-prepared drawings.

Equipment choices – for drawing individually and in teams

A whole range of equipment is available to help you when communicating ideas with drawings. Here we take a look at some of the main choices, including those with more advanced technology.

Ideally, choice will be guided by the method by which you or your group would like to present the drawings. Reality, however, may dictate that your choice depends on what is immediately available to you. One of the great advantages of getting used to 'live' drawing is that minimal equipment is required. As long as you have the idea in your head, you can explain it almost anywhere.

Big surfaces help teams express their ideas visually

Paper, notebooks, sketchpads, pen and pencil

Yes – your number one resource is good old-fashioned stationery.

- Great for practising and working out ideas.
- Sufficient to be able to explain an idea to someone with a sketch.
- Even A4-sized paper is large enough to present an idea to a small group.

Free-standing flipcharts

The flipchart is probably the most obvious and commonly available piece of kit for presenting drawings.

- Versatile – flipcharts can be positioned exactly where you want them.
- Select good quality paper – smooth white paper is recommended.
- Water-based chisel-tipped pens are recommended (rather than bullet-tipped) for thick and thin lines.
- Ideally a minimum of eight coloured pens are needed to give plenty of choice.

Whiteboards

The beauty of using whiteboards is that words and pictures created with 'dry-wipe' markers can be erased immediately, if necessary.

This allows you to make instant adjustments and variations to your drawings as you discuss them with a group or individual.

- Usually whiteboards use a landscape orientation – ideal for big drawings of processes or models.
- They are often fixed to office walls, so may be readily available.
- They are also available on wheels with boards that spin around – this increases flexibility in use.
- They require 'dry-wipe' markers that come in a variety of colours.

Interactive whiteboards

- These often are an electronic version of a regular whiteboard.
- Special pens are supplied.
- They are very versatile – for example, it is easy to switch colours, thicknesses of line or start new clean pages.
- Drawings usually can be saved electronically and often can be printed out in hard copies.

Facilitation boards

These are special free-standing boards that are excellent to use when facilitating group work. They come with backing paper that exactly fits the boards.

Their best feature is that you can stick card shapes onto this paper, yet take them off again and place them elsewhere on the board. This works because the boards come with glue that you spray lightly onto the surface. This makes the surface act rather like a sticky note. When you place a piece of card on the surface it does stick to it, yet at the same time you can remove it easily because the glue is not permanent.

This means that teams can write and draw easily on the cards (e.g. to illustrate a process), but then place them on the board and still move them as many times as they like to make adjustments.

Alternatively you can pin cards to the boards which gives equal flexibility of use.

- An amazing array of coloured card shapes are available with the boards, ideal for creating diagrams and models.
- Boards come in various sizes.
- Boards can be joined together to make very long areas for teams to work on.
- Boards and all required accessories can be hired instead of bought if you are using them only occasionally.
- Lightweight and free-standing so they can be moved easily around a room.
- Backing paper is usually available in white – which is great for drawing onto directly, or brown – which is an ideal contrast colour for the brighter coloured shapes on which teams can sketch and label their ideas.

Visualisers

A visualiser is a device like a video camera that will project images onto a screen.

- It enables you to draw on a flat piece of paper and lets people view your drawing projected onto a screen as you create it.
- It is adjustable, rather like an angle-poise lamp – this means it may be pointed at whatever drawing or object you want to project.
- You could, for example, point the visualiser at a flipchart and, just like a video camera, it projects what you are drawing onto a screen.
- It has the ability to connect to virtually any projector, interactive whiteboard, PC monitor or TV.
- Video and audio usually may be saved electronically.

Graphics tablets

These can be used to help you create drawings and save them in electronic format. Then they can be saved and incorporated into documents and electronic presentations.

- Special drawing pads can be linked to a computer, enabling you to draw on the pad and see the image emerge on the computer screen.
- They have an amazing variety of drawing media – for example, simulated pencil, brush, felt pen, crayon.
- They are extremely versatile with brilliant effects and features – for example, you can erase, build up layered drawings, and whole areas of colour may be blocked in at once.
- Fantastic quality of resulting images is possible.
- It is easy to save your work electronically.

Computers, tablets, tablet pcs and notebooks

There is an endless range of drawing features available on computers, tablets and tablet PCs.

- Many very portable devices are available so you can work anywhere.
- Many features of the graphics tablets will be available on these devices – and more in some cases.
- It is well worth exploring the vast range of options.

Practical tips for presenting 'live' with drawings

There are many things to consider when presenting a drawing 'on-the-fly'. I am a great believer in paying attention to detail because everything you do makes a difference. If you do enough things right, when these are all aggregated together the difference becomes huge. Sir David Brailsford, who achieved great success with the British Olympic cycling team, refers to 'marginal gains'. By this he means that excellence is achieved, not through doing one major thing differently, but doing numerous things really well. When all of these potentially small actions are aggregated they are sufficient to make a dramatic difference to performance.

Everything counts – attend to the detail

For this reason I will break down the process into different elements all of which are important if you want to achieve the best results.

Planning – work out the drawing idea in advance

You will make your job easier if you work out the following in advance:

- how the drawing will fit onto the surface;
- where to start the drawing;
- the sequence in which you will build it up.

Some people I have taught even use faint guidelines in pencil so that they can draw the picture accurately in front of the group. The guidelines usually are not visible to the group and, even when they are noticed, it makes no difference to the impressive effect of drawing 'on-the-fly'.

Positioning of yourself and equipment

Speaking position – the centre has the power

If you are speaking to a group, your impact is different depending on where you are positioned in relation to them.

The most powerful presenting position is in the centre

A chairperson at a meeting usually will occupy the central position at the top of the table. This is a far more powerful and influential position than that of those seated at the sides. It is where you will have the most impact.

Likewise, when you are explaining an idea with a drawing to a group or even an individual, you will find that the same applies. Therefore, if you are using a flipchart, position it so that you can occupy the central spot. This means that the flipchart is a fraction to the side of centre.

If you intend to draw on two flipcharts, then it will work best to position them equidistant from the centre. Then you can move to each as appropriate, knowing that you can always return to the centre, especially to make important points.

Place equipment so it looks and feels right

When speaking to groups there is always a position that is just right for the equipment:

- If you move a flipchart back or forward slightly it will affect your connection with listeners.
- You can tell intuitively when you are too near or too far away from people.
- They too have a sense of when you are just the right distance from them.

Adjust equipment to be comfortable for you – it makes a big difference

It is worth paying attention to this kind of detail. Just imagine a drummer at a concert trying to play when items of his equipment are not positioned quite where he likes them to be. Similarly, if you find yourself having to stretch too high, or bend too low to be able to draw, then this is not good. It will seriously affect your level of comfort and that in turn will impair directly your ability to draw effectively. There is also likely to be an adverse knock-on effect with your levels of confidence as well.

Small adjustments to equipment make a big difference when drawing

Therefore, take a moment just to check and adjust everything so that you can draw comfortably.

Presenting your drawing – the impact of words, voice and body language

Whether you are explaining your idea to one person or to a large group, we cannot talk about creating the drawing in isolation. This is because the message you deliver when speaking to people will comprise the following elements:

- the drawing itself;
- the words spoken;
- voice qualities (e.g. tone, pitch, intonation, emphasis, pace);
- body language (e.g. eye contact, gestures, facial expression, posture).

All of these will combine to affect how your message is received. Therefore, these four elements play a part in conveying your message. They need to be in harmony if you are to get your message across as you intend it. If those elements are not in harmony, then those listening will receive a mixed message.

Your words, voice and body language must give a consistent message

Tips to get your ideas across

Here are some tips to get your ideas across when drawing.

Timing and other tips

Go for short 'live' drawing inputs – just a few minutes

One of the best ways to maximise the effect of 'live' drawing is in shorts bursts. Just a one- or two-minute sketch as an introduction to a meeting, training course or coaching session can really grab attention and set the scene.

Equally, a quick sketch in the middle of a traditional electronic presentation can have a very high impact. You could reserve your sketch for an idea that is central to your presentation. This can help you to make your point in a concise, yet engaging, manner.

Even for the more detailed drawings, such as models and visual maps, drawing inputs of no more than 5–10 minutes typically work best.

Take your time

If you rush a drawing you are likely to make yourself more nervous and this will transmit itself to those watching. Professional sportsmen and women who are at the top of their game always seem to have plenty of time and make it look easy. The same applies to communicating with drawings. You can go slower than you might think because people will be absorbed in following your drawing as it emerges.

When you take your time:

- you will feel more calm and in control;
- it will be easier for people to follow; and
- you will create a better looking visual.

The words – have a practice – it helps create the story

The words and the drawing need to go together to create the story. The best way to ensure that they do is to have a run through. By this I mean to actually try explaining your idea to yourself, or a colleague, whilst drawing the picture. This is an instinctive approach that works really well.

The benefits of this approach are as follows:

- You will learn the best sequence in which to build the drawing.
- The act of drawing prompts words that naturally go with the picture.
- You will come up with new and useful ways of explaining the idea.
- You will find out quickly if parts of the drawing or explanation are more challenging.

- It will act as a good rehearsal, enabling you to refine further if necessary.

Voice – use it to add impact to your message

The way we say words can easily alter their meaning. We have all had the experience of hearing people say a reluctant 'yes' in a tone that really means 'no' or 'I'm not sure'.

'Yes, I'm really excited about that'

Therefore your voice needs to match your words if people are to receive the message as you intend it.

Use your voice to help convey the true meaning of your drawing. You will do this most naturally by:

- matching voice energy to desired mood (e.g. serious or light-hearted);
- emphasising key messages contained in the drawing;
- varying pace and volume to maintain attention.

Position yourself so you can see everyone

The first thing to ensure is that you position your flipchart in such a way that you can easily turn to see the audience. This means not having your back to the flipchart but instead standing side-on in such a way that makes it easy to draw, but also easy to turn to the group. The same applies when using whiteboards or any other surface upon which you are drawing.

Make eye contact to increase rapport

When drawing 'live' naturally you are focused on what you are drawing. However, this does not mean ignoring those watching and listening. Making eye contact is an important way to connect with people and build rapport.

Therefore, break off drawing now and then to make eye contact. As you make eye contact, this is an ideal opportunity to:

- explain an element of your drawing;
- invite a response;
- emphasise an important point.

Include everyone in your eye contact

It is important to include everyone in your eye contact because if people are excluded they tend to feel left out. With larger groups it is not possible to look at people individually, but you can achieve the same effect by looking at sections of the audience. As you look at a section, people get the sense that you are looking at them individually. In this way you create a positive connection with them.

Look where you want people to look

It is important to make sure that people look where you want them to look. In this way you keep them focused on either yourself or the visual. This is much better than allowing them to look wherever they want, because this results in fragmentation of attention.

Spike looks where he wants the audience to look – they will always follow the speaker's eyes

Believe it or not, when you are speaking, people tend to look in the direction that you are looking. You may have noticed in everyday conversation that, when you are speaking to someone if you glance behind them, they will also look around. In fact, the visual cue is so strong that it even overrides an audio cue. This can be demonstrated by looking directly at a group and asking them to look to the left while you are still maintaining full eye contact with them. They find this really difficult to do. What tends to happen is, despite asking people to look away, they keep their gaze on you because the visual message is stronger than the auditory one.

You can use this principle to really great effect when drawing while speaking to a group. All the time you are looking across at the picture the audience will look there too. When you turn towards them their eyes will look back to you. In this way you can easily control where they will look. The reason why this is so important in presenting is that it is really helpful to have full eye contact with the audience when making certain points. For example, when you want to make an important point it is best to look directly at the group. In doing so you will deliver your point with full impact.

Stand upright for confidence and credibility

Your ability to draw well in front of a group is affected directly by how you feel. If you are nervous then this will not only adversely affect your own confidence but also will have an impact on the group's response. People will pick up easily on signs of anxiousness.

One of the quickest ways to change your state is to change your physiology. Just try smiling and feeling unhappy now at the same time. It is actually impossible to do.

Likewise, when you want to be in a confident state, your posture makes such a difference. If you stand up straight with your feet about hip width apart you will not only start to feel more confident but also you will look more confident too.

Change your physiology to change how you feel

When we change the way we sit or stand we change the way we think and feel

Breathe deeply – to relax when speaking and drawing

You may have noticed that when people are nervous often they have shallow breathing too. This is a vicious circle because by not breathing properly they become more nervous.

However, if you stand up straight with feet evenly balanced and take several deep breaths you will cause changes naturally in the body chemistry that increase feelings of confidence and calmness. This often is called being 'centred' and is a very resourceful state. The simple act of being aware of your breathing brings you into the present moment. When you are fully present you are much more able to connect with the group and will be able to speak and draw much better.

Use gestures – but put the pen down when not drawing

Using gestures to explain ideas actually makes it easier for people to understand us. It is also the case that we can flow much more because we find our words more easily when we use gestures as we speak. When I run professional presenting courses I often do an exercise where I ask people to speak whilst keeping their arms still and at their side. They find it surprisingly difficult to do and discover that their words do not flow as easily as when they allow their arms to move. Therefore, if you use gestures, you will find advantages for both yourself and your listeners.

Gestures are more effective and easier to do without a pen in your hand. It means you have both hands free and can do open-handed gestures that look natural. This will help you when you want to turn to the group to make key points.

Furthermore, when we keep a pen in our hand there is also a tendency to fiddle with it, which can be a distraction when speaking to groups. Therefore, putting your pen down when not actually drawing will be beneficial all round.

Make it a two-way experience – how to really involve people

If we are to keep our audience engaged it is important to deliver our talk in a way that feels much more involving and is a two-way experience. When we do this the experience for the audience is much more active rather than passive. We will now examine a number of effective ways of doing that when we are using drawings to present ideas.

Keep them guessing

One way to keep people interested is for them to be trying to figure out what you are drawing, or about to draw. Therefore, anything you do or say that gets people curious about what is coming next is helpful.

You do not even have to ask them questions in order to get them thinking. The fact that you are drawing 'live' should do that for you.

However, you can always say a few things that will heighten the chances that they will take a guess at what is coming next, for example:

- 'I am about to illustrate the biggest barrier to growing our business.'
- 'Guess what the main thing is that customers like about us?'

If you keep the guessing principle in mind, you will find ways to involve people naturally as you draw.

Ask questions – allow the group to contribute ideas and increase engagement

The simple act of asking questions is the most obvious way to involve a group in your presentation. However, if you are trying to get a concept across to the group you may not want your input side-tracked. Therefore, ask questions only where the responses will be helpful to you and will move your talk in the direction you want.

Open questions are helpful when you are happy to receive a lot of information:

- 'What is important about this part of the process?'
- 'How could we achieve that?'

Closed questions are helpful when you want a 'yes' or 'no' response:

- 'Do you think that would work?'
- 'That's worth trying, isn't it?'

A closed question can help you to gain the group's agreement at the end of a key point.

Ask rhetorical questions – to enhance rapport

There is great benefit in asking rhetorical questions as you proceed with your drawing. Even though you are not expecting an answer, these questions still prompt a reaction from the group. Furthermore, if you ask questions to which the answer is 'yes', this would result in building up agreement between yourself and the group. This, in turn, will increase the level of rapport between you and group members.

Rhetorical questions are useful when you want a 'yes' response, e.g.:

- 'Do you find there are some people with whom you just "click" immediately?'
- 'Have you noticed that the item you really like is always just a bit more than your budget?'

By being flexible in using different types of questions, you can really enhance the level of rapport and engagement between yourself and the group or the individual to whom you are presenting your ideas.

Check their understanding – do they have questions?

Keeping your eyes on the reaction of the individual or group will give you a good idea of how well they understand you. You may, however, wish to check now and then if they have questions. Alternatively, if you prefer not to have questions until you have finished, simply ask the audience at the start to keep any questions until the end.

Let them finish sentences as you draw – keep them involved

You can do this quite easily, as you are about to draw certain items. In other words, just stop short of drawing the item and let them call out what they think you will draw and say next.

This works best when the end of your sentence is fairly obvious:

- 'In any situation there are not only advantages but also …'
- 'When something goes up, of course it eventually has to …'

When someone gives the answer, you can draw an appropriate symbol and write the word.

Use the 'call and response' technique

This is where, instead of saying a word or phrase, you get the audience to say it back to you.

This can help you to reinforce a key message that you have presented already. The fact that the audience is able to say it instead of you reinforces the fact that they already know it. Let's look at an example.

Imagine that you are speaking about health and safety and the key message is that people need to keep their eyes open for suspicious people or behaviours. You have come up with the key phrase 'always be looking'.

Assume that you have already introduced the phrase and drawn a pair of eyes as a memory jogger.

You might say, for example:

> *'The consequence of someone leaving a suspicious package in the store is potentially disastrous and that's why we need to...'*

and trust the audience to say,

> *'... always be looking'.*

Simply pointing to the picture or phrase on a flipchart often is enough to get the response. This is a very effective way in which a drawing can reinforce key points.

Potential problems of 'live' drawing

There are some things to watch out for when drawing 'live' but, with a little preparation, you can avoid these easily, or deal with them if they do occur.

The drawing not fitting onto the surface

By this I mean that you embark on the drawing only to realise that you have begun it in such a way that you are going to run out of space. This is not usually an issue with very simple drawings. It is more usually a problem with drawings that involve a number of elements and perhaps some detail.

Causes

This problem usually is caused by one or both of two factors:

- starting in the wrong place on the paper;
- starting the drawing too big.

Solutions

- **Start again.** If you are actually presenting when this happens you are usually aware of it quite early and can tell that you are heading for a problem. It looks much more professional simply to start again and do it properly than to end up with an unsatisfactory picture.
- **Prevention** is the ideal, of course. Practice and repetition is the key to it. Practising on the same size surface will, almost certainly, prevent the problem occurring in the first place. Often you will find that, if you try the drawing just a couple of times, you will become aware of any problems of scale and be able to iron them out.

Forgetting parts of the drawing – or not drawing them well enough

Forgetting what you are going to draw is just as problematic as forgetting what you were going to say in a presentation. Whilst people may tolerate the odd lapse, it usually is a certain way of appearing unprepared and unprofessional.

Causes

The most common causes are:

- not having memorised it properly in the first place;
- just having a mental block – we have all had experiences of our minds going blank.

Solutions

- **Draw it a couple of times in advance.** We actually remember better if we do the drawing rather than just see it. This is sometimes referred to as 'muscle memory' and is certainly the way to go.
- **Draw the picture in the same sequence each time.** This makes the muscle memory even better and means that before long the drawing becomes automatic. Think about when you write your signature. Most people will write it the same way each time. This means that probably they could do it with their eyes closed. They are actually familiar with the feel of it and they can do it almost without conscious attention.
- **Do an extra practice of any elements that you find tricky.** When you have trouble with a drawing it is usually only a part of it that is challenging. Once you are aware of this you can simply practise that part a couple of times.
- **Have a copy of the drawing handy.** Always keep a copy of the drawing nearby so you can have a look if you are stuck. If you have it there, the chances are you will not need it.

Keep a copy of your drawing where you can see it

How to get teams drawing

If you ask a room full of people 'who can draw?' you will typically get only one or two positive responses. Most of the reasons for people saying they cannot draw are to do with belief rather than skill. The majority of people have not had a positive experience of drawing and are convinced it is beyond them.

How do we convince people to draw in a team session?

There is no one answer to this question. However, there are a number of things that you can do all of which will help to get people to the point where they are prepared to have a go. Different things will convince different people and therefore, by using a number of different 'convincers' and reasons, you are more likely to get everyone on board than when just one reason is given.

Some teams will already be naturally more open and creatively minded than others and may need little encouragement to pick up a pen and draw. The following guidance is for teams where this is not the case and they need some convincing and encouragement to take part.

Let us look at what you can do easily that will help people.

Give some reasons why drawing can be helpful in communicating their ideas

Most people will be willing to give it a go if they can see a reason for doing so. You can use some of the ideas in this book to make the case, for example:

- A picture is worth a thousand words.
- The drawings do not have to be brilliant to communicate an idea.
- Drawing can help us to develop our ideas.
- It can help us to share our ideas with colleagues and understand each other better.

For most teams a brief practice or warm-up will suffice

Recognise that what you're asking might seem a bit different. Therefore, give them some valid reasons why drawing will be helpful for communication.

Having a practice or warm-up is usually sufficient to get people into the idea of using drawing skills.

Choose from some of the activities that you have learnt in this book to give them the idea that there is a basic visual toolkit.

Practice and warm-up ideas

- Drawing Spike.
- Drawing stick figures.
- Drawing basic shapes, lines, arrows.
- Drawing symbols to represent ideas.

In my experience, even a few minutes of warm-up will do the trick for most groups. You will also find many excellent ideas and practical techniques for working visually with teams in David Sibbet's book, *Visual Meetings*.

Tips to enhance team sessions using visual communication

An informal room set-up

It is amazing that rooms can feel different depending on how they are set up. People get a feel for the atmosphere as soon as they walk in. It is easy to appreciate how different levels of formality can be created simply by how the room is arranged.

There may be times when you have little choice or can make only minimal adjustments. On other occasions you may have free rein to arrange a particular set-up such as for a team workshop or meeting.

Let us take a look some of the choices.

Cabaret set-up

An informal cabaret or café-style arrangement is often ideal when encouraging people to express ideas in drawings.

For a group of 12 one might imagine 3 round tables with 4 people seated at each. Then flipcharts and/or facilitation boards may be placed around at the front, sides and back. This allows groups to have plenty of space between them.

Boardroom set-up

Usually this will have a more formal feel to it and therefore may not seem ideal for team drawing work. However, even if groups start by being seated at a boardroom table, it is quite easy to get them up on their feet and working at facilitation boards or flipcharts placed around the room.

Tables arranged in a horseshoe shape

This is a traditional set-up for some training courses. It can also have a rather formal feel to it. However, like the boardroom arrangement, once you get people up and out of their seats you can create a much more informal atmosphere.

Good size surfaces for visuals

There is often a chicken and egg relationship between the materials and equipment available and the visuals people will produce.

We have already discussed equipment such as flipcharts, facilitation boards and whiteboards. The key thing is to ensure that they are in sufficient quantity and of sufficient size to allow people to draw comfortably. If people are trying to cram pictures onto small surfaces it is not ideal. Having large enough surfaces is also important for presenting ideas back to make it easy for people to see.

In the absence of large boards for drawing it is possible to join flipchart sheets together to create larger surfaces.

Good range of attractive and good-quality drawing materials

Attractive and good-quality drawing materials often will inspire people in their creations. In other words, materials will, to an extent, inform the different methods and techniques people may employ.

I have already spoken about having a good range of colours of water-based chisel-tipped pens. However, I would recommend having thin felt-tipped pens too, again water-based. It can be really handy to have thinner markers. I have noticed that people find them very useful even when creating large diagrams or maps because they sometimes need to draw certain items smaller or wish to label certain parts with smaller letters.

Music to enhance energy and productivity

The first thing to say is be careful if you use music as it can be entirely inappropriate in many business settings. However, there is no doubt that music creates states and moods and therefore it is worth considering for group work. An occasion when it is more readily accepted is when a team gets together for a facilitated workshop or training session.

I have found that when people are working in groups on drawing activities then the use of baroque music in the background works well. I have used many pieces by composers such as Vivaldi, Handel and Bach, playing them quietly in the background or even a little bit louder at times. There is much research concerning the use of certain music that points towards its positive effects in connection with learning and productive working. Personally, I avoid using music with lyrics whilst people are working and stick to instrumental pieces.

Much baroque music tends to have around 60 beats per minute, equivalent to the average resting heart rate. This creates a state of relaxed alertness which is good for learning and productive working. If music is very slow then it will induce a soporific effect. Similarly, extremely fast music may be just too upbeat in most cases. As you try different pieces you will get to know what works for you.

Just have a go and see the positive results

Providing you are well prepared and have thought through what you are doing, you will find that groups always produce something positive when asked to represent their ideas in drawings. It is something that they really enjoy and often they surprise themselves by coming up with unexpected and creative results. It really is just a matter of using the ideas and techniques we have discussed. Once people are up and running then there is no stopping them.

Furthermore, when groups see for themselves how much drawings help them to express their ideas, they too will be convinced that the use of drawing skills is highly valuable. The trick simply is to get them started and be willing to have a go. Therefore enjoy introducing the drawing techniques to groups and be ready to be amazed at the innovative ideas and visual representations they come up with.

Enjoy developing your ability to communicate using drawing

You will be the best judge of whether you choose to do drawings completely 'live', partly prepared or completely prepared. It may be that you use a combination of all of these. Your choice may depend on your level of confidence in being able to carry out a particular drawing successfully. It may also depend on what you believe will work best in terms of creating the best impact.

Whichever approaches you choose, the great thing is that you have a range of options each of which will help you to convey your ideas in memorable pictures.

You will be amazed how, with practice, you can very quickly develop your confidence at drawing ideas while explaining them. Some key things to remember:

- Do not wait until your drawings are perfect before using your drawing skills 'in public'. Remember that the drawings do not have to be perfect, just good enough to get your idea across.
- Most of all, enjoy presenting your ideas with a sketch because your positive energy will transmit itself to those watching and listening. When you are enjoying explaining an idea it is much more likely to be engaging for the group. Likewise, the more you can see that the group is engaged, the more your confidence will increase.

Summary

- Choose from pre-prepared, partly-prepared or 'live' drawing approaches.
- Pay attention to detail – everything counts.
- Plan your drawing in advance.
- Have a run through before drawing 'live'.
- Maintain an upright posture for confidence.
- Look where you want the audience to look.
- Make eye contact with people.
- Involve those watching – make it two-way.

More practice

Have a go at explaining an idea with a picture.

Here is an excellent chance to practise. Ideally, it would be great to choose a real example, such as an idea you need to explain to an individual or group.

If you do not have a real example right now, you could select something from any topic familiar to you. It may be work-related or a leisure subject.

In either of the above cases it might help to find a willing volunteer who will watch you have a practice once you are prepared.

- Write down the main subject heading.
- Write down the aspect you are talking about.
- Notice what pictures pop into your mind.
- Sketch the pictures.
- Think about how you would include the picture in an explanation.
- Decide if you would draw the picture 'on-the 'fly' as you speak, partly-prepared or completely prepared.
- Now have a go at explaining it to someone or a group.
- Get some feedback on what you did well and any ideas of what you could do differently next time.

The power of two visuals

By 'two visuals' I mean showing two separate pictures on the left and right. Below we see Spike using two flipcharts.

Representing time – it feels natural for most people to see the past to the left and the future to the right

Alternatively, if you have only one visual surface such as a whiteboard, this could mean splitting the picture as Spike has done below.

In this way you can represent numerous contrasting concepts or visually represent ends of a continuum. I am not recommending doing this all of the time. There are many benefits from having a single picture or

screen for people to focus upon. However, the use of two visuals is a very powerful device for achieving many additional benefits.

Why two visuals?

All too often presentations are simply about conveying information. This is all very well when our objective is purely to inform. However, there are many instances in which we need to win over the hearts and minds of people. In such cases we need to convey more than just information in order to get people on board.

Whilst a logical argument is extremely helpful, people often need a connection at the emotional level in order to create a shift in beliefs. Emotional connections mean that people actually feel differently about something and, when this happens, we can really make progress in bringing them with us.

Naturally there are many aspects of presenting that can help us to do this. Hearts and minds are won over in all sorts of ways (e.g. a dramatic story, a startling statistic, a powerful quotation). In addition to all of these, one very effective device to assist us in such shifts is the use of two visuals to help people move from one emotion to another. It also happens to lend itself to a great application of our drawing skills.

There is a whole range of states that we may want to create (e.g. curiosity, intrigue, concern, anxiousness, surprise, confidence, calmness, excitement and many more). In this chapter we will see that with our two visuals we can easily begin to show contrasting ideas. Two contrasting ideas can trigger contrasting feelings which can help us make our points in a convincing way.

Let's look at some examples and see how they work

Metaphors are really useful for describing opposites. The contrast between the two pictures helps to make the two ideas memorable. The pictures also evoke different feelings.

- current scenario
- threats
- dangerous waters

- new marketplaces
- opportunities
- safe ground

The example above shows how visuals can help you to do the following.

1. Accentuate contrasts so distinctions are sharper and memorable

By placing contrasting concepts on either side of a room we can accentuate their differences visually. They are spread apart visually which means that people can grasp such distinctions more easily compared with just explaining them or placing them on one picture together.

2. 'Anchor' concepts to specific locations and feelings

By placing a concept on one side of people's visual field you are effectively creating an association between the concept and its location. Furthermore, it allows you to associate concepts with feelings, for example, problems with negative feelings and solutions with positive feelings. In other words, we are 'anchoring' the feeling to the concept and the location. By doing this we have created powerful connections, which help people understand and relate to our ideas.

3. Represent a timeline visually which makes understanding easier

If you asked people in an audience which side of the room represents the past naturally they will point to the left. Likewise, they will tell you the future is on the right. This is so instinctive and also consistent with other conventions. For example, we read from left to right. Similarly, if we were to draw a numbered line from 0 to 100, we would label it with 0 on the left and 100 on the right.

For this reason, representing the past on the left and the future on the right makes complete sense to people. This means that you are communicating in a way that is easy for people to follow. If you represented it the other way around, people may or may not notice consciously, but it just would not feel as natural.

4. Switch attention fast and easily

A great way to keep people engaged is to change their focus of attention. When we change attention we can change the rhythm of a presentation. Just like a piece of music, when the rhythm changes it creates interest for the listener. The change of attention can act as an energy spike to keep people engaged.

What this means for you is that it is fast and easy for you to refer back to an idea by just looking at it, gesturing towards it or moving back to that location when you talk about it.

As you move back to that location, people more easily associate with that concept. For example, if you had problems listed on the left-hand flipchart, the moment you return to stand by it people start to associate easily with that aspect of your talk.

The great thing for the audience is that, by keeping the left and right flipchart content visible, they are able to see everything all the time. This helps them to maintain the sense of where you are moving from and where you are heading towards.

5. Tell your story – take people on a journey

When we want to persuade people about an idea, usually we are taking them on a journey from their existing thinking to a new idea. However, people are not always easily persuaded to accept something new. This is where using our two visuals is an incredibly effective device for taking people on a journey with us. Our two flipcharts can help us to show people the benefits of moving from their current thinking towards a new idea.

People find the story format so easy to absorb. Our two visuals on the left and right lend themselves to us being able to present our ideas in a story form. It is easy to see that, for example, we could move from problems on the left to solutions on the right via a story. Even a couple of very simple visuals can be enough. For example, on our left-hand flipchart we could have images of disappointed customers. We could then present our ideas for solving the situation. Then we could have on the right-hand flipchart a list of those future actions to improve the situation along with images of happy customers.

6. Create powerful introductions – for meetings, presentations or workshops

The two-visual technique can help you to make great introductions. By referring to the two pictures you can easily give people a brief overview at the start of a session. For example:

- Left – this is where we are now.
- Right – this is where I want us to get to.

- Left – here are the problems.
- Right – this is the desired outcome.

- Left – this is the old way.
- Right – this is the new way.

One could imagine many other examples where it may be helpful to create that immediate contrast right at the start.

More examples of two contrasting visuals

- challenges
- cons
- fears

- opportunities
- pros
- hopes

- negatives
- problems
- bad news

- positives
- solutions
- good news

- theory
- the concept
- wisdom

- practice
- application
- next steps

- past
- then
- old

- future
- now
- new

- ideas
- insights
- thoughts

- actions
- tasks
- to do

Practical tips on presenting with two visuals

Stand left, right or middle

Now we will look at standing position choices. Our decisions will be informed by what we are trying to achieve and the effect we wish to create.

The centre is the most powerful position – best for key messages

As described earlier we can use the two visuals technique for:

- representing time;
- accentuating contrasts and making distinctions sharper;
- anchoring concepts to locations;
- switching attention.

Whilst we have set up visuals left and right for the above purposes, as I have mentioned already the central position is the one for highest impact when presenting. What this means for you is that, even when using two visuals, you will find the centre to be a very effective place from which to deliver really important points. Therefore, do use the centre in addition to your left and right positions.

In choosing where to stand the principle is incredibly simple:

Stand by the relevant visual to reinforce its point

If you have started a talk by placing visuals on the left and right to represent past and future, then it will be important that you present from either one of these two points or in the centre. This will make your presentation much clearer visually and make it easier for people to follow.

One of the key purposes of setting up the three positions is to affect the state or feeling of the audience. The reason for doing this is that, in terms of motivation and persuasion, we want to be able to affect changes in how the audience is feeling about what we are saying. A key thing to be careful about is to be precise in where you stand because you want to enhance the visual and the message it conveys.

The following pictures show the potential set-ups and options for where to stand. For the purposes of the example, I have used 'past', 'present' and 'future' as the key positions. However, the same idea will apply if we use the positions to visually represent other concepts, such as those shown earlier (e.g. problem/solution or cons/pros).

- **Using a whiteboard or facilitation board – with pictures split.**
  Here you have the chance to stand to the left, right or centrally in front.

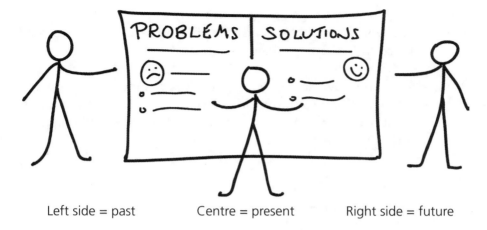

Left side = past   Centre = present   Right side = future

Variations – one could create some variation to this, for example:

- **Using two flipcharts.** In this instance you could stand at the left flipchart, centrally or at the right flipchart.
- **One flipchart.** In this example you are confined to one flipchart and therefore would need to draw/show the first picture and then turn over the flipchart page to draw or show the second.

We therefore need to keep in mind the potential benefits of the two pictures and how our positioning and movement can help us to achieve those benefits.

Use words that match the state you are trying to create

The actual words we use can make a massive difference to the way people are feeling. We know that, when spoken, certain words evoke feelings in people. Therefore, with careful attention to our words, we can begin to create a state or feeling in the room that will enable people to get on board with us.

Some words automatically evoke more negative feelings, which can be helpful in highlighting the pain caused by problems you want to solve. Connecting people to the pain of a problem increases motivation to find a solution. You could also use words that get people intrigued as a way of motivating them to listen further.

Similarly, if you want to get people into a solution-orientated state, you can use words that help to achieve that and cause them to feel much more confident and positive.

Imagine that you have set up your two visuals, showing a problem picture on the left and solutions on the right. Let's look at the kinds of words that accentuate the contrast between the two and begin to communicate the state associated with each.

Describing problems

When describing problems you may use words like:

> *concerns, issues, worries, difficulties, issues, hassles, disappointments.*

As you use such words immediately you begin to communicate those kinds of feeling to the listeners. What this means for you is that they are not only getting the information but also they are getting a little of that negative feeling too. This emotional connection is valuable because it is a negative feeling that people will be motivated to get away from. In other words, they will be ready to go with you as you begin to talk about potential solutions.

Describing solutions

When describing solutions you may use words like:

> *easier, better, successful, confident, progress, results, exciting.*

Therefore, also with a little attention paid to the kinds of words you are using in conjunction with your pictures, you will find that you will get an emotional connection more easily. As you use the more positive words you can see the effect simply by watching the group's faces becoming more positive. By really watching them you get feedback on how well you are doing at creating the desired state.

Use voice and body language that match the two contrasting states

I have mentioned earlier that the quickest way to change your state is to change your physiology. This is especially useful when presenting either of the two contrasting visuals.

When you change your physiology, your voice qualities and energy tend to follow. Imagine, for a moment, sitting with your head in your hands in a rather forlorn manner. Your voice and energy will tend to match that posture. By contrast, if you sit up straight and smile your whole energy will change to become much more positive. The audience will pick up on your state and be influenced by your energy.

Therefore the rule is as follows:

Adopt the desired state to match what you are talking about.

For example, if you are at the left visual talking about concerns or complaints, it will help if you adopt a concerned manner yourself, not only in the words you use but also in energy, voice qualities and body language.

When you move to the right-hand flipchart to talk about solutions and positives, it will be important to adopt an upbeat energy, voice and body language to match.

In this way you enhance the power of your drawings and any words you write or display to the audience. In doing this, everything is working in harmony so that people get the full message as you intend it to be received.

Look and gesture towards the desired visual

As I mentioned earlier, people will look where you look. This is particularly helpful when using two visuals, especially when you are on one side of the room and need to refer to the visual on the other side.

Instead of having to walk back to the other side, you can get people to focus on it simply by looking towards it and even gesturing to it.

This is a quick way to switch attention from one visual to the other and another reason for having two pictures visible at the same time.

Use two visuals to ask for contributions from the group

In addition to presenting ideas, the two-visual technique is also great for asking the group for their contributions.

Standing by the flipchart on the group's left you can draw your picture or symbol at the top and write the word or pose a question and ask for the audience's contributions.

By remaining next to that flipchart as you write, you are 'anchoring' the audience's contributions to that side of the room and to the feelings that those comments evoke.

Once you have written up these contributions, you can move to the centre to explain what happens next. This is taking you visually from the problems/issues and concerns of the past into the present. In making that movement you have dissociated yourself from that negative state. As you stand in the centre you are accessing a more positive state. The great thing is that, even from that central position, you can always refer back to the flipchart without actually getting into the negative state again.

As you now move on to asking the group for ideas/positives/solutions, etc. you are able to draw and write easily on the flipchart to the audience's right. When you do that, their visual focus will have changed to 'the future' and, in doing so, the audience's emotional state also begins to change in a positive way. Furthermore, you are in the brilliant position of now having set up the anchors in the room. You can, therefore, move back easily to the central position to make key points. You can also gesture to one flipchart or the other from that position.

Keep your left right and central positions distinct

Using two flipcharts to get the group to draw/ write their ideas

We can use the same anchoring principle to get the group to write up ideas themselves. One of the benefits of asking the group to do it is increasing ownership. When people actually write the ideas themselves they are even more connected to them. Another benefit is that getting people up on their feet can break up your presentation in a positive way by getting them more involved.

Again it's important to keep the flipcharts anchored in two distinctly separate places to represent, for example, past/future or problems/ solutions as before. If you do not have two flipcharts, you could simply have flipchart paper on one wall representing the past and on another wall representing the future. All you need to remember is to keep them the right way round, moving from left to right.

Potential problems of using two visuals – what to be careful about

As I have explained, there are powerful reasons for using two visuals, not least the ability for you to take people on a journey towards the outcome of your presentation. Add to that the emotional power of visual anchoring and you really do have a valuable technique at your disposal.

However, you may be wondering whether there are any potential risks or downsides. As ever the answer is that it depends on how you actually present whilst using your two flipcharts. I have already given quite a number of tips but in this section I will seek to highlight some important dos and don'ts that can make a big difference.

- **Don't wander about without purpose when presenting:** If you start wandering about or speaking from other positions, you will not be maximising the potential of the visual set-up that you have created. Furthermore, people will find it distracting and will be less able to easily follow what you are saying.

- **Don't use two visuals unless you have a clear purpose for doing so:** It is important to use two visuals when you have a reason for doing so rather than just as a gimmick. When used with a specific purpose in mind they are extremely effective.

- **Do be flexible in your stance – be ready to change it for a purpose:** Naturally, when we are drawing pictures we are going to be side-on to the group. Our stance is likely to be somewhat informal or casual whilst drawing. However, this does not preclude us from adopting a more confident, assertive stance when we turn to the group and especially when we want to make a key point.

Enjoy experimenting to maximise the power of two visuals

The recommendations given in this section will give you a solid basis on which to further develop your skills. Through practising and experimenting you will develop and refine your skills and get to know instinctively what works best for you.

Summary

- Use two visuals to emphasise contrasts (e.g. past/future, problems/solutions).

- Place visuals left and right – then people associate each idea with its location.

- Stand left, centre or right – don't wander or stand in between the three positions.

- Stand in the centre to talk about the 'present' when explaining past/present/future.

- Use words that match the feeling you want to create, for example, 'anxious', 'apprehensive' or, conversely, 'excited', 'positive'.

- Deliver key messages from the centre for maximum impact.

- Combine sketching with electronic presenting on occasions when using both will add value.

More practice

Have a go at these work-related issues using two visuals.

- Identify a work-related issue that has two sides to it. Make it the kind of thing that you might reasonably have to explain to an individual or a group at work. For example: negatives and positives; problem and solution; past and future; old methods and new methods.

- Take two sheets of paper – place them side by side in front of you.
  - On the left-hand sheet write some words and draw some symbols or pictures that could represent the negatives, problems, past or the old – or whatever issue you have chosen to represent on the left-hand picture.
  - On the right-hand sheet write some words and draw some pictures or symbols that help to represent the positives, e.g. the solution, the future or the new – or whatever you have chosen to represent on the right-hand picture.
  - Select the best symbol or picture from each of the sheets.
  - Now re-draw your two selected symbols or pictures onto new sheets of paper and, if needed, write any words to go with them.
  - See if you can get an opportunity to try this out by explaining it to an individual or group.

Making key messages memorable

Strong key messages

One secret of making a presentation memorable is to have a really strong key message. The key message will be something that stands out, yet is supported by the detail of your presentation.

Effective key messages tend to be:

- concise;
- easy to understand;
- memorable.

Advertising is full of memorable key messages that fulfil those criteria:

- 'Just do it' – Nike.
- 'Your country needs you' – wartime recruitment campaign in the UK.
- 'Five a day' – health campaign to encourage people to eat fruit.

When it fulfils these three criteria, the chances are that you will make your message stick successfully. Repetition of the key message in different ways is another method of getting it across.

Why draw your key message?

When you are presenting to a group they will not remember everything you say. What you need to be certain of, however, is that they remember your key message. Perhaps you have a call to action which is important that everybody understands. If your message is captured in a memorable picture this will help to ensure that it sticks. If you can draw all or some of the picture 'live' then you will also add to its impact.

Once you have the picture drawn, make sure you have it constantly visible allowing you to refer to it whenever you need. It also provides a focal point and makes it easy for you to talk about your message and to gather additional ideas from the group.

Using metaphors adds impact to key messages

Metaphors are an integral part of the way we speak. When encapsulated in a picture they can really help people to remember your spoken words. As you read the three examples below, just notice what happens to your thoughts and feelings:

- 'Don't throw the baby out with the bathwater.'
- 'We are not out of the woods yet.'
- 'We are running to stand still.'

Key messages often contain metaphors – making them memorable

We will explore the power of metaphors in more detail in the next chapter, but keep an eye out for examples as we now explore further key messages.

Types of key messages

It is helpful to think about different types of key messages. Sometimes you simply may want to inspire people, or perhaps you are interested in making sure they do something specific. It may be that you want to highlight the essence of a problem for your organisation or perhaps point the way towards the future.

Let's look at some examples of different types of key message and ways to make them memorable with pictures:

1 **Pearls of wisdom** (e.g. famous quotes or your personal gem of wisdom).
2 **Calls to action** (e.g. asking for a specific behaviour or quality of thinking).
3 **Highlighting a problem** (e.g. the current situation).
4 **Showing the way to a solution** (e.g. the strategy for success).
5 **Fascinating facts** (e.g. where a fact helps support a key message).

Let's look at examples of each type and how they might be conveyed in a drawing.

Have a go

Have a look at the following examples and draw the pictures below. As you draw, see what other pictures come to mind and draw those too.

1. Pearls of wisdom

'Don't be afraid to take a big step if one is indicated. You can't cross a chasm in two jumps.'
David Lloyd George (1863–1946), British Prime Minister

'Logic will get you from A to B – imagination will take you everywhere.'
Albert Einstein

2. Calls to action

'Keep your eyes open for every opportunity'

'We need connected thinking'

3. Highlighting problems

'There is no safety net'

'There is no turning back'

4. Showing the way to a solution

'We need to be great jugglers'

'We need to grow our people'

5. Fascinating facts

Facts can be sparks for creating key messages or ways of illustrating them. Therefore, one way of coming up with key messages is to find a fact that is relevant to it.

Here we see how a fact can be used to create a key message and provide a memorable picture.

The sub-four-minute mile

Until Roger Bannister ran a mile in under four minutes, many people believed it was impossible. The fact that this was a belief that limited performance was illustrated when shortly after he achieved it, a number of other athletes also ran a mile in under four minutes.

This is a very useful story to make a point about the power of belief.

A simple drawing with a written key message makes it memorable.

'If we believe it, we can achieve it'

Here is another example of using facts to reinforce key messages. Despite the fact that man started flying planes only around the early 1900s, a man landed on the moon well within the same century. This fact could be used to support a number of different key messages, for example, 'It's amazing how quick progress can be.'

'It's amazing how quick progress can be'

Where to use key messages in a presentation

One of the important things about a key message is that you want it to be memorable. It's a known fact that people tend to remember things that are:

- first;
- different;
- last.

First – primacy

People very easily remember things that come first and there are numerous examples in everyday life. Ask yourself when did you first meet your best friend? Or what was the first drink you had today?

The same applies when asking people to remember information, such as lists, when you will find the first word often is very easy to remember.

Different – the isolation effect

When so much information is competing for attention it is natural that much of it is filtered out. However, it is known that an isolated item will attract attention. The 'von Restorff effect' was named after psychiatrist Hedwig von Restorff (1906–62). She found that items that stand out like a sore thumb are much more likely to be remembered than other information. We tend to remember the unusual or distinctive. This might be unusual facts, striking quotes or highly colourful and vivid images.

Last – recency

We also remember things that are last, or the most recent in our experience. For example, you can easily remember the last meal you had. What was the last journey you made? Where was the last place you saw your best friend? All of these are easy to answer and the principle is applied easily in presentations by including things that you want people to remember at the end of your talk.

Tips to get your key message across

Include it in a story

The key message itself can be introduced first with a story in the form of an example or business case. You may tell this whilst doing the drawing or showing a pre-prepared picture. The story format is a memorable one and a great way to ensure people remember your key message.

Stories are great to help you deliver key messages

The key messages often can be really obvious in the story, which is very helpful. However, drawing the picture can create a powerful association with your story that will keep it in the audience's mind.

Be brief – less is more

Brief but dramatic experiences stay in our memory for a long time. Similarly, you will create more impact when you can contain your key message to a brief input. If you are introducing it through a story, you would be amazed how well a very brief story or anecdote can work. A short story with a good picture can give great impact to your message.

Repetition makes ideas memorable

Repetition is great for memory, but there is a balance to be struck between repeating a message in order to reinforce it and saying it too often. However, you will be able to repeat your message effectively if you do so in relation to a new point or fresh evidence that you are introducing. In this instance it makes complete sense to point out to your audience how the information you have just given contributes to the overall key message.

Repeating a message at the end of sections is also a useful time to emphasise it.

What if I have an electronic presentation?

It may be the case that the bulk of what you want to say is contained in an electronic presentation. However, this does not preclude you from introducing your key message with a 'live' drawing. On the contrary, to do so injects a change of pace and produces a positive state in the room. This has the benefit of creating variety for the audience and also making your key point stand out from the rest of the presentation.

There is also nothing to stop you also having your key point within the electronic presentation. Having drawn it on a flipchart, you can keep it visible throughout whilst still proceeding with your electronic visuals. Furthermore, you can even have a professional-looking picture in an electronic presentation that is a version of what you drew informally on a flipchart.

Putting it all into practice – get the 'key message' habit

Next time you are creating a talk, have a go at deciding right up front what is the key message you want to get across. Decide whether it is simply an important and inspirational message to remember or whether it is a call to action. Then see what images come to mind as you think about it. Ask yourself what metaphors, stories or examples would illustrate your key message. Also try to craft the message itself in different ways until it has an impact. Sometimes key messages lack emotional impact. Therefore, see if you can achieve a form of words that gives a good feeling as you read it. If you do this, the chances are that you will come up with a good image to go with it.

Another key tip is to try coming up with a number of alternative images. What you will find is that you always come up with one that is easier to draw than the others, yet still has the same impact.

The main thing is that your picture is visually powerful enough to carry your key message and make it stick in the minds of your audience.

Summary

- Keep your key messages concise, easy to understand and memorable.

- Use pearls of wisdom, calls to action and fascinating facts.

- Use metaphors to add impact to messages.

- Highlight problems and solutions with key messages.

- Present key messages at the start and end of your talk to ensure they are remembered.

- Repeat key messages during a talk to make them stick.

- Keep your sketches of key messages visible throughout to ensure they are absorbed.

More practice

Illustrate a key message:

- Write down one key message that relates to your work or that of your organisation.
- Sketch some of your ideas that could represent that message.
- Redraw the best one and write the message to go with it.

Metaphors and similes

In the previous chapter we saw examples of the usefulness of metaphors in key messages. We will now explore them further, along with similes. Metaphors and similes are such a part of everyday language that it is almost impossible to have a conversation without hearing them or using them ourselves.

A **metaphor** is defined as a figure of speech that contains an implied comparison, for example:

- We *are* skating on thin ice.

A **simile** explicitly indicates that one thing is similar to another, for example:

- It's *like* a sprinting race.

Metaphors and similes really do lend themselves to the expression of ideas in pictures. This means that they are an ideal way to share thoughts and ideas.

Use a metaphor as an introduction to a talk or a meeting

You can use a metaphor to great effect as an introduction to a team meeting or talk. It is a brilliant way to get your main idea across right from the off. Keeping your drawing visible will ensure that your metaphor is kept in mind throughout.

Get your team drawing a metaphor to show how they see it

For teams, metaphors are an excellent way to explore issues in real depth and a brilliant way for colleagues to share their thoughts.

Draw a metaphor to show your key message

A quick sketch of a metaphor may take only seconds, yet the impact can be immense. Once you have created that picture it will stay in the memory of those watching,

Why sketch metaphors and similes?

Here are just some of the numerous reasons why metaphors and similes are useful:

- They are hugely rich in information and a picture is a great way to convey that richness.
- They are a really quick/shorthand way of making a point.
- You can ask excellent questions that encourage the group to examine, refine and further develop the metaphor.
- They are extremely memorable.
- Often they evoke feelings so that people get an emotional connection.
- They focus the group on your key point.
- They are extremely powerful vehicles for exploring problems and ideas.
- Naturally people will find meaning of their own in metaphors and similes.
- Once presented, people will always see more detail in a metaphor from their own point of view.

Let us explore in more depth just why metaphors work so well.

Metaphors are multi-sensory

A key reason why metaphors and similes work so well is that often they contain a variety of multi-sensory information. By this I mean that they help us to access all of our senses.

Metaphors stimulate our experience in many ways and, when described, often they contain many sensory-specific words. A small sample of such words is as follows:

- **Visual** – seeing (e.g. look, clear, vision, bright, dark, foggy).
- **Auditory** – hearing (e.g. loud, silent, quiet, ringing, harmonious).
- **Kinaesthetic** – feeling or movement (e.g. touch, crunch, smooth, rough, sharp, hot).
- **Olfactory** – smell (e.g. aroma, pungent, acrid, smoky, perfumed, scented).
- **Gustatory** – taste (e.g. delicious, sweet, bitter, hot, spicy, refreshing).

It is in their appeal to the senses that metaphors often carry their power.

Dry information versus the emotion of metaphors

We can convey information in a very dry and digital manner simply by stating it. However, metaphors provide so much more than just the information itself in terms of message impact. They provide an emotional impact and connection. For this reason alone they are so effective in communication.

The following pairs of statements show the difference between simply stating a fact and using a metaphor, which evokes pictures, sounds and feelings.

- *'This is project is very difficult'* versus *'We're spinning plates.'*
- *'We are very busy at the moment'* versus *'Our feet aren't touching the ground.'*
- *'He's thinking about it'* versus *'I can hear the cogs whirring.'*

Examples of metaphors expressed in drawings

Take the following example. Imagine that you are managing a team and you want to get the idea across that it is important to have ongoing feedback on performance.

Giving feedback on performance

We can liken the process of giving feedback on performance to sending a rocket to the moon.

There is constant feedback between the rocket and mission control

You could draw the picture starting with the earth and mission control. Next you could draw the moon and then the rocket on its way. This would help to explain that constant feedback is necessary to make ongoing adjustments to the trajectory of the rocket.

In the following picture you will see that I have added arrows. The smaller arrows would be drawn first. The first small arrow shows a very slight movement off course with the next arrow indicating an equally fine adjustment to keep the rocket on track. The subsequent small arrows show the same. The point being made is that every time the rocket moves even a fraction off course, a small adjustment is made immediately to get it on track again.

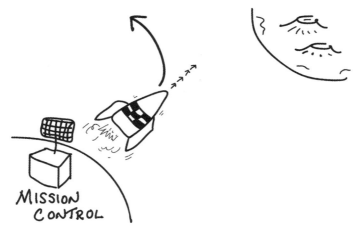

If we did not make the small adjustments early the rocket would veer well off course

One could then draw the big arrow to show what would happen if ongoing feedback was not received and acted upon. The rocket would miss the moon by a long way, as shown by that arrow. The resulting gap between the rocket and the correct path to the moon would be enormous.

Then one could liken this process to giving feedback at work. If it is not given little and often, performance can go way off track and then be hugely difficult, if not impossible, to recover.

Therefore, this is a very graphic way to make that point. Not only that, as you can see, it lends itself to being drawn 'live' because you can reveal the story and your key points gradually and with more impact. In this example you have a very simple, but powerful, way to make a point.

Have a go

Have a go at a quick sketch of the rocket to the moon picture. It is all basic shapes and lines.

Let's have a go at some metaphors

The following exercise will give you practice at drawing and also thinking in pictures.

Have a go

I have already drawn a picture for each metaphor below.

- Draw each picture.
- See what other pictures come into your mind for these metaphors. This could be a variation on the pictures I have done or totally different pictures.
- Now draw your own variations or new versions.

'We are in shark-infested waters'

'We are all singing from the same hymn sheet'

'Fortunately we have a reserve parachute'

'We are pushing a bus uphill'

'We are firefighting'

'I'm snowed under'

Similes work just as well

Similes work as effectively as metaphors. In fact, with a slight change of language, the metaphors above could have been written as similes.

Let us do a couple of examples.

Have a go

Draw my examples below and then draw alternative pictures of your own that come to mind.

'It's like staring into the abyss'

'It's like keeping all the balls in the air'

As you can see from these examples, the drawings can be quite simple and yet still get the idea across.

Getting a team drawing metaphors to express their ideas

In addition to drawing metaphors yourself, it is a great idea for teams to make their own drawings to express their ideas. The actual quality of the drawing is not as important as the fact that it enables them to explore and communicate their ideas in a very effective way.

You could ask groups to draw a metaphor to represent, for example:

- the problem... or the desired outcome;
- the current situation... or the desired future;
- the process at the moment... or what it could be like;
- the service we currently provide.... or how it could be improved.

Groups can draw their metaphors by working individually, in pairs or in sub-groups or whole teams and then present their drawings to colleagues to explain their ideas. This is not only a creative way to explore issues and topics but also a way of communicating very quickly and effectively because a powerful metaphor says so much.

Using questions to explore and develop a metaphor

We can explore the metaphors further within a group by asking questions to yield more information.

When you use questions to help a group explore or further develop their metaphors, there are a few key points to bear in mind. One thing to be wary of when asking questions is that you are not putting forward your own ideas disguised as questions. There may be nothing wrong with that, providing you know you are doing it. However, it is all too easy to ask the group a question in such a way that you are actually putting your own content into their metaphor. So what are the alternatives?

One method is to ask questions in a way that may be described as 'clean'. There is a whole field of study on the subject of 'clean language', which is concerned with helping people to explore issues without adding in your own ideas. The kinds of questions I have suggested below originate from the work of David Grove, as developed by James Lawley and Penny Tompkins and documented in their book *Metaphors in Mind*.

Let's take an example: the metaphor is a crossroads

In response to the question: 'What metaphor describes where our business is at the moment?' someone might reply, 'We are at a crossroads.'

x WE ARE HERE!

Examples of clean questions or lines of enquiry could be the following:

'What kind of a Y is that?' (Y being the metaphor) – so in this instance one could ask, 'What kind of a crossroads is that?'

The above question would elicit more information, which may help the individual or group to enrich the metaphor. In doing so they would be getting more detail about the situation.

'Is there anything else about that?'

This question encourages the group to look for anything that may be missing. For example, in this instance: *'Is there anything else about the crossroads to tell us?'*

'What's beyond that?'

Once the metaphor is drawn you could ask questions that may help the group to understand the relationship between what they have drawn and other potential elements. In this instance one might enquire, *'What is beyond the crossroads?'*

'And what happens just before that?'

This question will encourage the group to explore time and examine what occurred just before the part of the journey they have drawn.

In this instance it could be, *'What happens just before we get to the crossroads?'*

'What happens next?'

This question also explores time. This may encourage the group to explore potential solutions. In this example we might enquire as to *'What happens next?,* i.e. when we move from the spot marked X on the picture.

Once you have a metaphor illustrated it will prompt all kinds of questions and reactions. It is, therefore, a very useful vehicle (excuse the metaphor), for exploring issues.

Make the most of metaphors

You can see just how useful metaphors are. They can really connect with people at a deeper level than plain information. They often convey the real feeling and emotion of a situation. The fact that they are so useful in presenting an idea and also in group work makes them an especially valuable tool. They will certainly stimulate the imagination and creativity of groups.

Summary

- Use a metaphor or simile as a shorthand to explain your thinking.

- Draw a metaphor as a powerful introduction to your talk.

- Keep your metaphor drawing visible so it is a constant reminder.

- Ask teams or individual members to draw a metaphor to show how they see, for example, a problem, process or vision.

- Use 'clean' questions to help a team or individuals explore and develop their metaphors.

More practice

To reinforce and develop your skill at drawing metaphors and similes, have a go at any of the following that apply to you:

- Think about the organisation that you work for. Write down a metaphor that would describe it. Or it could be a simile: e.g. *'Our organisation is rather like...'*.
- Think about your career; what metaphor would represent where you are at the moment?
- Think about a current issue or problem in your work; what metaphor would represent that issue?
- Think about a project you are working on, in or out of work; what metaphor would describe it?
- Draw a picture to show any or all of the above.

Business models and processes

At times you may need to explain a business model or process. Or, perhaps, sometimes you are required to actually develop a model or encourage colleagues to do so. Either way, the use of drawing skills is really useful to be able to get ideas into a visual form. Once you have the ideas expressed visually, it makes them easier to share with others and to develop further.

In fact, drawing skills are helpful in all kinds of ways when working on any of the following:

- models;
- theories;
- new ideas;
- processes;
- visions;
- strategies;
- action plans;
- problems or obstacles;
- solutions.

These could be concerned with all types of business topics, for example, management models, behavioural styles, communication models, performance-coaching models, finance, sales, marketing or production. You can use drawing skills to illustrate an existing model or process or one that you are currently creating yourself.

Why do drawings help?

All the benefits of drawing mentioned hitherto are relevant, especially the following:

- **Building a story.** You can bring your model or process to life by building it up like a story. Writing the words and drawing the symbols as you explain it works really well because people gradually see your ideas develop.
- **Adding pictures makes it less dry and academic.** Some models and processes can come across as very dry and academic. However, when you draw the model and add pictures, it becomes much more engaging and easy to absorb. It can even be entertaining and it will make you and your model memorable.

Drawing 'live' is ideal – but even pre-prepared pictures can work well

I would suggest that wherever possible you use 'live' drawings. However, the use of pre-prepared and partly-prepared drawings can also work very well. There may be times when you do not feel it is practical or possible to draw everything as you speak. If a model is very detailed you may decide to have at least part of it drawn in advance.

What formats work best?

When communicating a model, idea or process it is important to choose a format that will make it easy for you to explain and easy for people to understand.

Sometimes the best format is obvious and the more common ones include:

- simple four-box grid;
- four-box grid with labelled vertical and horizontal axes;
- flowcharts – in various configurations;
- continuum – horizontal lines.

It may be that your idea fits none of these, in which case it may work best to improvise and create your own way of arranging your idea visually.

Let's look at these formats with simple examples to illustrate how they work.

Simple four-box grid

The simplest idea of a four-box model is where there is literally one square divided into four. The following is an example.

The four Ps of marketing model

This model, originally developed by E. Jerome McCarthy in the 1960s, highlights key areas to consider in marketing:

- product;
- price;
- promotion of the product;
- place of purchase.

In this example we need just four boxes because we have four key points. Nothing is written on the vertical or horizontal axes in this instance.

Building a story with this model

It can be seen easily that the pictures could be drawn completely 'on-the-fly' or just partly drawn beforehand. For example, one might simply draw the squares in advance or perhaps just some elements of the pictures and then complete the rest in front of the group. All you need to do is to decide in which sequence you are going to build the story. Then it is simply a case of elaborating on each section as you move around the model.

Have a go

Have a go at drawing the model.

Now let's look at a four-box example that has horizontal and vertical axes.

Four-box grid with axes

This is a very common way of building a model where two ideas or concepts are taken and placed on the vertical and horizontal axes. It is, in a sense, more complex than the previous version in that one is able to explore the relationship between two ideas. This is achieved by using the boxes to show the four permutations and also their resulting effects.

Ease/impact model

In this model, the purpose is to explore the benefits of taking various actions to improve a situation or solve a problem. This kind of model is used frequently in continuous improvement workshops to separate out ideas and help to decide which ones to go ahead with first.

The four boxes could be created on a facilitation board and people could write ideas on cards and stick them in the relevant quadrant. A whiteboard and 'dry-wipe' markers would work equally well.

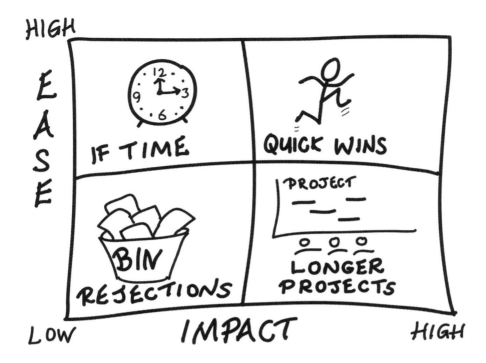

Easy-to-draw pictures make a model memorable

As you can see, 'ease' is represented on the vertical line with the 'high' end reserved for actions that are very easy to implement. Likewise, the 'low' end is for actions that are less-easy. Similarly, on the horizontal line we see 'impact' shown with 'low' on the left and 'high' on the right. This then forms a matrix with criteria by which people can judge their ideas.

I could have drawn any number of simple symbols or pictures. The key point is that the illustration just needs to be an appropriate link to the meaning in order to be effective.

Have a go

Have a go at drawing the above model.

Building the story of a four-box model with axes

We can see that it would be easy to tell the story of this model by first drawing the vertical and horizontal lines and labelling them. As with many of these models, the top right box is highly desirable and often the one that people see as the most productive to pursue first.

Typically, as with many other such models, you could:

- explain the bottom left box;
- then proceed to top left;
- then bottom right;
- finally arriving at top right.

Explaining the boxes in this order enables you to really build the model to show increasing benefits in terms of ease/impact. You end up with actions that are really easy to do yet have great benefits.

The symbols are so simple that they can be drawn 'live' easily as the story builds. There is ample opportunity to discuss further implications of the model with the group as one is building it up.

If you are unsure about your ability to draw all of the elements, it is easy to see that some of these could be partly pre-drawn. You could still retain some of the benefits of drawing 'live' but add other parts as you speak.

The principles used in this example can be applied to drawing and explaining numerous other models.

Variations on horizontal/vertical axes models

There are, of course, endless variations that can be created, based upon the idea of the four-box model. The next model we will look at is an excellent illustration of this point. In addition to four ideas being generated by the vertical and horizontal axes, you will see that a central idea is represented along a diagonal channel:

The flow model

This example is from the book *Flow: The Psychology of Optimal Experience* by Mihaly Csikszentmihalyi.

I am using this as an example of how models can be explained and brought to life by means of adding simple pictures. I have purposely drawn simple figures of the kind that we have been learning.

The model illustrates what the author describes as 'flow' activities. These activities are those in which we are, typically, totally absorbed. We concentrate in such a way that we are totally immersed in the experience. The model shows how levels of performance can be increased when we are in what he describes as the 'flow channel'.

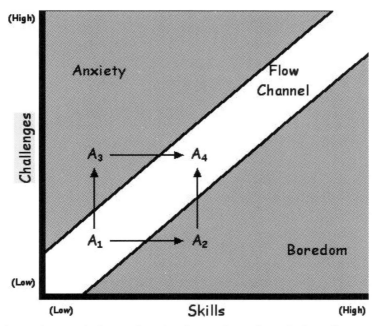

From *Flow: The Psychology of Optimal Experience* by Mihaly Csikszentmihalyi
(page 74)

Here is the model again with my illustrations added:

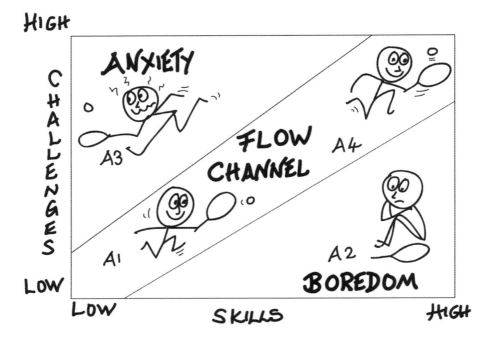

You will see that the two axes represent levels of skills and challenges of the performer of the task.

In his book, Csikszentmihalyi uses the example of a boy called Alex who is learning tennis. You will see four points on the model, A1, A2, A3 and A4, which represent him engaged in tennis activities at different points in time:

- **At point A1** he has almost no skills and his key challenge simply could be to hit the ball over the net. He is shown as being in the flow channel here because the level of difficulty is just right for his limited skills.
- **At point A2** you can see that he has become bored because after a while his skills improve and the original task becomes too easy.
- **At point A3** he finds himself in a situation where the challenge is just too high in relation to his skills (e.g. playing a much more skilful opponent). This causes some anxiety. In order to get back into the flow channel the challenge needs to be reduced.

- **At point A4** he gets the right amount of challenge again and this requires a higher level of the skill. Despite the increased complexity, as long as the activity does not overstretch him he will remain in the flow channel.

Building the story of this model

In this instance the model itself dictates what might be the most sensible order in which to explain it. It would be straightforward to build up a narrative around this model with the examples whilst drawing the pictures in each box. Even if one had the pictures drawn in advance, it would still be a way of fixing this model in the memory.

Using the same idea for other models

Once you get into the swing of thinking in pictures it becomes quite easy to think of simple pictures or symbols that can represent elements in a model such as this.

Have a go

Have a go at doing a quick sketch of this model and see how easy it is to do.

Improvising with axes to create your own four-box models

It is easy to improvise and create four-box models with vertical and horizontal axes to create variations of your own. Once you have two labels for the axes you are able to create the model.

Here I am improvising with the words 'creativity' and 'actionable'.

Imagine that you want your team to come up with ideas for a new product or service. You also want to be able to judge the ideas in terms of whether they are creative or actionable or, ideally, both.

By placing the two words on the vertical and horizontal axes, as shown below, you can see that extremely simple symbols can be used to represent the ideas in the four boxes.

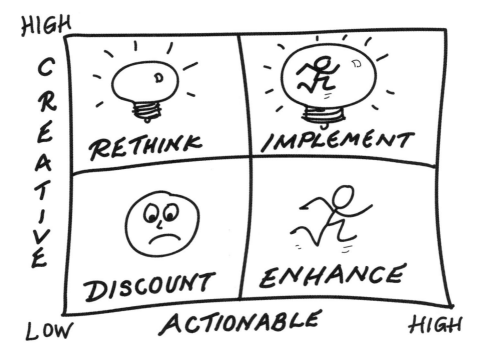

As you can see we have:

- bottom-left box = neither creative nor actionable;
- top-left box = highly creative but not very actionable;
- bottom-right box = highly actionable but not very creative;
- top-right box = highly creative and highly actionable.

In my example, you can see that I have decided to combine the light bulb and running figure in the top right-hand box. Notice also that I have placed a word in each box. This is to suggest a choice to discount, rethink, enhance or implement ideas, depending on the quadrant into which those ideas fall.

Have a go

Draw a quick sketch of the model above.

Building the story of this model

This model lends itself to being started at the bottom left and finishing at the top right.

Flowcharts to communicate models and processes

Next we will move on to take a look at flowcharts, which are excellent ways to represent models and processes. We examine some examples and I would like you to focus on the simplicity of the drawings and how easily the processes can be drawn.

Flowchart example – delivery process

It is easy to see the process and recall the picture to remember it

This is a flowchart that shows the process used by a delivery company to get a parcel from the client's offices to the customer's home. Notice how simple the pictures are and one can, therefore, imagine how easy it would be to draw these at the same time as explaining the process. By keeping the drawings simple it helps not only the audience but also yourself. Use of colour would help further to make the picture engaging and memorable.

Have a go

Just have a go at drawing the model.

Linear horizontal flowchart example – interview preparation

You can see that this is the kind of process that simply might be explained across a whiteboard. I have kept the symbols as simple as possible, yet they are certainly good enough to assist me in explaining the process. You can see that it would be very easy to build a story around this process. Once drawn on the board it is easy for the presenter to refer to the stages.

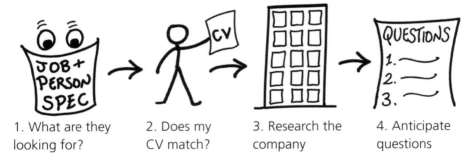

1. What are they looking for?
2. Does my CV match?
3. Research the company
4. Anticipate questions

You can see from these examples that flowcharts can be used to represent all kinds of things. It is easy to imagine using an office whiteboard in a meeting to sketch out all kinds of processes for discussion.

As with all our drawings, the use of different colours will also help to make images and words stand out. This becomes even more important if we end up with a lot of information on a flowchart. Colour coding information and using different sizes of drawings and labels really does help to make more complex processes easily understandable.

Continuum models

There may be times when you need to explain ideas that can be represented easily on a continuum. In these instances you may want to draw attention to either end of the continuum, or any point in between. In such cases, a picture or symbol to accompany the label at either end is an effective way to make it memorable.

Here are some examples:

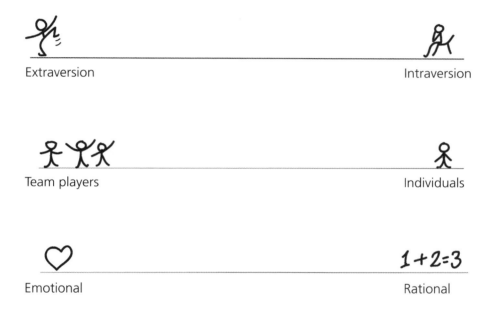

Extraversion   Intraversion

Team players   Individuals

Emotional   Rational

One can imagine using the same idea to represent many other concepts at either end of a continuum.

Free-flow drawings to express your own ideas

It may be that you have something to explain that does not fit a particular template. In these cases it is a good idea to improvise and create a way that works well for you.

You may, for example, be able to explain an idea on a whiteboard simply by arranging symbols or pictures without the need for any particular framework.

Have a look at the different examples that follow. You will see simple symbols joined up with arrows and labels.

You can see from this example that it is easy to show the relationships between elements within an overall model or process. Such diagrams could be drawn easily on an office whiteboard for a team to discuss. The act of drawing the picture in itself inspires discussion and enables groups to critique ideas.

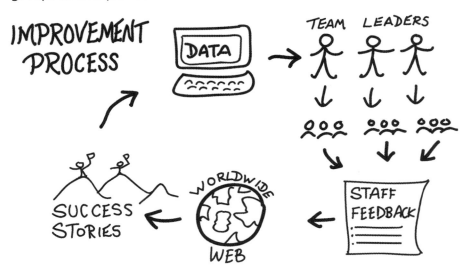

It is easy to create your own pictures to explain processes and models

In this example you can see many of the symbols that we have drawn before. They are all easy to draw, yet convey the information perfectly well.

The picture almost explains itself. All the presenter would need to do is to elaborate on each section in order to bring the whole process to life.

An example created by a business client

Here is an example based on one created on one of my presenting workshops by a woman who wanted to explain a job reporting process.

The purpose was to show the original process and then add a new line (dotted) to show the shortcut that had been created. She had drawn the model in advance but then added in the extra line as she explained it.

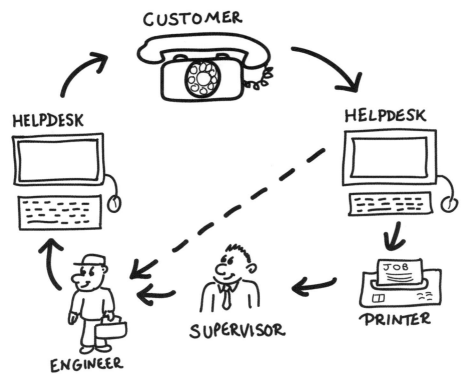

My client created this chart to show the shortened process of fixing faults

The process starts with a customer reporting a fault to the helpdesk. As you can see, the helpdesk then needed to print the job details. The whole purpose of the talk was to explain that, at this point, the job can be held up and then to show how she had made it quicker.

The problem in the system was that job details may sit on the printer for some considerable time before being passed to the supervisor.

Another time lag may happen between the supervisor and the engineer who needs to receive the details in order to complete the job.

She went on to explain that, in order to solve the problem, the information would now go directly from the helpdesk to the engineer's mobile phone. This would cut out the need for the printer and the supervisor to be involved in the process.

In order to show how she had removed the problems and shortened the timescale, she then drew an arrow in a different colour, shown with a dotted line, from the right-hand helpdesk right across to the engineer. In this way both the printer and the supervisor were helpfully cut out of the process.

The way she did this was so simple, yet so effective, and certainly conveyed the solution very impressively to the group in a very short time. The act of drawing the shortcut line 'live' graphically illustrated the saving of time.

Use cards or sticky notes to build a model

As an alternative to drawing as you go along, you could pre-prepare sticky notes or cards to stick onto a surface. By using lots of different colours and drawing pictures clearly on them and writing labels you can create a very effective series of images.

Tips on presenting any kind of model

For creating and presenting business models visually you really must:

1. Build the suspense

Starting with a blank sheet you have a great opportunity to really captivate people. You will be missing a trick if you do not make every effort to keep them wondering what is coming next.

2. Take your time to keep it tidy

I have sometimes drawn a model in front of the group only to look at it and realise that I could have done better. It is not necessarily that the model was terribly drawn, just that with a little time and care I could have made it clearer. Therefore, make sure that the various elements are well-placed in the drawing. Print clear labels that are a good size to read.

3. Use contrasting colours

Make the model easy on the eye. This is especially important when you have a lot of information. For example, you may have a label at the top and the bottom of each of four boxes meaning eight words in total.

Once you add in a picture as well, this can end up looking rather crowded. The simple act of colour coding labels can really help. You might as well for example, have headings at the top of each box in blue and labels at the bottom of each box in red. This then begins to separate out elements for the viewer and makes it much easier to understand.

Give copies of models to the group

Having presented the model, it may be useful for people to have a copy and naturally there are various ways to do this.

Give copies of your hand-drawn version

The great thing is that having drawn the model it is very easy for you to capture a picture of it for everyone. People might even decide to take a picture of it themselves. When they take a photograph of what you actually drew it will bring back the memory.

Give copies of an original version

This may apply where the model you have chosen to explain already exists in a printed form. There may be a case for providing a copy of this as well, especially if it contains additional written detail that you did not show on the version that you drew.

What about drawing a model and also showing an electronic version?

One of the benefits of drawing a model in front of the group is that because you are explaining it you may not need to write a lot of information on the flipchart or whiteboard.

There may be times when it can be useful to supplement your hand-drawn overview with a more detailed electronic version. In this way you can be doing a presentation that incorporates the benefits of 'live' drawing alongside the more usual electronic format.

Just have a go and try things out

My tip is just to begin experimenting with ways of enhancing your style of presenting models to groups. You might start by looking at an existing model that you present and thinking up some simple symbols or icons to go with your written words.

Even the simplest of symbols done in the right way with appropriate colour is enough bring a word or label to life and make it easier to recall. You will be amazed how even very straightforward pictures will hold the attention of the audience as you explain your model.

You will also get used to incorporating drawings while you are explaining models. You will get accustomed to a pace of delivery that works for you and is also right for the audience. So enjoy having a go.

Summary

- Use words and pictures together to make models and processes memorable.

- Stick to one-word labels where possible for simplicity.

- Use colours to highlight key elements of business models and processes.

- Sketch your own free-form models and processes.

- Encourage groups to use drawing skills to show existing models and create new ones.

- Use the most logical sequence to explain four-box models.

More practice

In order to build your skills at thinking in pictures for models and processes have a go at any of the following:

- Identify an existing model or process that is of interest to you. Draw a sketch of the model but add in pictures that would help explain it to others.

- Identify a process that is relevant to your work. Just start drawing and create a picture to illustrate it.

- Think about the business model for your own organisation. Draw a sketch that you could use to explain it to someone else.

Bringing graphs and charts to life

Why draw a graph when you could just show an electronic version?

Many graphs are perfectly well presented electronically. In fact, there are so many excellent ways of building up graphs and charts in electronic presentations. The ability to add and subtract elements, create moving elements and animation really does give plenty of scope to make graphs interesting in electronic format. My advice is to keep using electronic means of presenting graphs when it makes complete sense to do so.

However, if you want to present a graph in a different way with more compelling effects then why not draw it?

Do both

The two methods are not mutually exclusive. One might imagine situations in which you may draw some graphs or charts by hand whilst presenting others electronically. You could even present the essence of a graph by drawing yet also have a smart electronic version with all the detail as an additional slide or printed document.

Keep them engaged

When you draw a graph yourself, as you speak, you have a huge degree of control in terms of keeping people engaged. You are well-placed to create a dramatic effect to illustrate a trend or result such as a dip in profits or sharp increase in production. This is really helpful if you think of a graph or chart not as a set of data but rather as a story. Consider that you have a story to tell and that the graph is there to help you.

Switch their focus

It is very easy to switch attention between yourself and the graph or chart when you are actually drawing it. As you draw the graph and look at it yourself, the group will also focus on it. Then as you turn to the group you can regain eye contact in order to deliver key points with impact.

A great technique is to use two flipcharts when explaining graphs: draw the graph on one flipchart and make further points on the other. The benefit here is having both displayed simultaneously so that you can explain how the information on one visual relates to the other.

Line graphs

Whilst any graph is capable of being drawn by hand, some graphs lend themselves to drawing by hand more than others.

Line graphs can sometimes seem more static or more difficult to interpret when the whole picture is presented at once. Your drawing skills will enable you to create graphs before the very eyes of the audience. This means you can create curiosity and intrigue as the story unfolds. Drawing the graph yourself gives you complete control over how much of it you reveal at a time. This is therefore, a brilliant way to capture attention and interest.

Typically, line graphs are excellent drawn 'live', especially when you want to present the impact of trends over a period of time. The act of drawing a line going up or down is so much more powerful than seeing it already prepared. Equally, when we have several lines on a graph these may be drawn in different colours as you tell the story of the data you are presenting.

If you have a lot of complexity on the graph, however, it may not lend itself to being hand-drawn.

Line graph example – fitness graph

The line graph drawn here is ideal for drawing as you explain. It shows that, when someone first begins take a programme of exercise, fitness levels increase very quickly but thereafter we find there is a plateau effect.

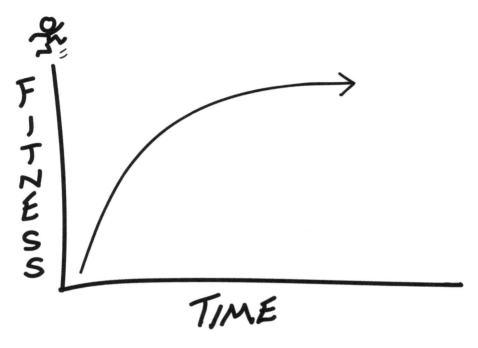

A really quick sketch drawn 'live' is all you need to explain this idea

This type of line graph may be used for all kinds of other topics such as:

- sales of the product at first launch, which then reaches a plateau;
- initial costs of a project which are high over the short term then tail off;
- learning curve when introducing a new person into a project;
- property values over time;
- seasonal effects of tourism;
- profit over a period of time.

Comparisons on one graph

The great thing about drawing something like this 'live' is it really does make it easy to add variations such as dotted lines (or lines of different colours) as in the example below.

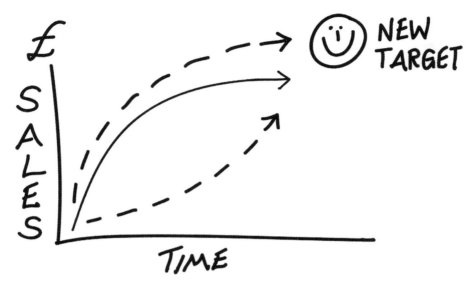

It is easy to bring comparisons to life with a freehand sketch

Different coloured lines may be used to show comparisons such as:

- sales trend of one product versus another;
- comparison of marketing costs over time between two products;
- the benefit of taking one action versus another.

These may be added spontaneously as you discuss various 'what if' scenarios with your audience. The beauty of drawing such a graph by hand is the flexibility it gives you to illustrate variations in the moment.

Drawing two graphs to show a comparison

Sometimes there is a case for drawing two graphs because it is easier to make a more striking comparison. In this case graphs may be drawn either one above the other or on two separate flipcharts.

This example is about presenting to a team in a training session. The key point is that typically we are more attentive and remember more at the beginning and end of a session. This is because of the principle of 'first' and 'last', which I mentioned earlier.

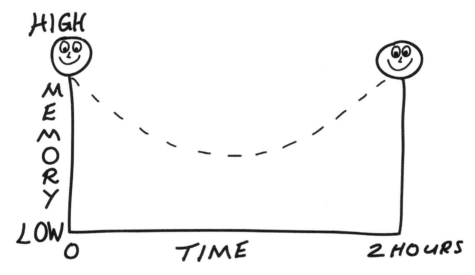

Showing a fall in attention and memory over time lends itself to a quick sketch

To illustrate this point, the graph above shows a two-hour period allocated for the training. The horizontal dotted line is high at the beginning of the session, showing that people are likely to remember more near the start. It dips in the middle and is high again at the end. Therefore, in this example, there is *one* 'first' and *one* 'last' and these are shown by circling the beginning and the ending of the session. The total of 'firsts' and 'lasts' in this training session is, therefore, *two*.

Now a second graph shows how to improve on the ability of people to be attentive and remember information in the same time span.

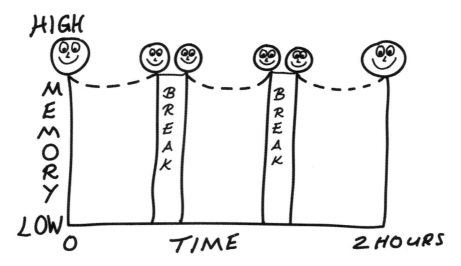

In this second graph you will see that two short break times have been added within the two-hour period, thus creating three shorter sessions.

As each of these sessions has its own beginning and end we now have a total of *six* firsts and lasts, which are illustrated by the circles. Therefore, we have more times when attention and memory is likely to be better. It can also be seen that attention does not dip as much in these shorter sessions. This, therefore, is a very quick and informal way of illustrating such a point.

Pie charts

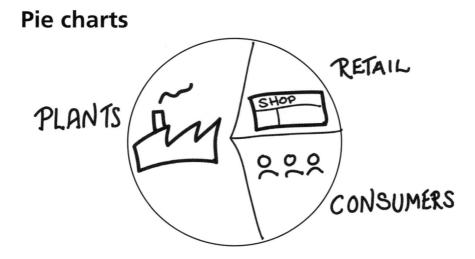

Depending on the point you want to make, there may be a case for drawing certain pie charts by hand. This is especially true when you want to create a degree of suspense as you build up your story to make a dramatic point.

Simple pictures make it possible to build up pie charts with quick sketches

Naturally you could still do this electronically by having different sections appear one at a time. However, actually writing the words or drawing symbols by hand really does mean you can synchronise your speech closely with the visual as it develops. Not only that, but, as we have discussed previously, the act of drawing lines, symbols and writing words really does grab attention.

Here is another example showing how even simple drawings will work well.

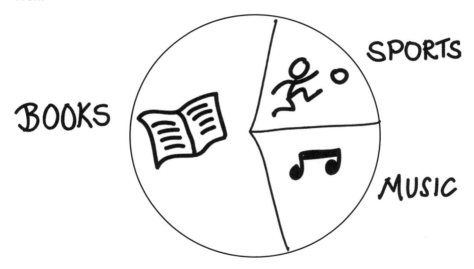

As you can see, even quickly drawn symbols are enough to make an effective visual.

Block graphs

Block graphs (e.g. histograms) may have vertical or horizontal bars. These can be presented so well in electronic format that, in my view, it is much more difficult to a make a case for drawing them by hand. There may, however, be some situations where drawing by hand can be useful.

You may want to draw a block graph by hand when:

- the point the graph makes is rather dramatic and you feel that this impact can be conveyed really well when you draw the bars 'live';
- you want not only to draw the graph but also add other lines and notes to it as you speak;
- the graph is so simple that it lends itself to a quick sketch;
- no electronic means of presenting are available.

Here are some examples of histograms.

Histogram example: sales

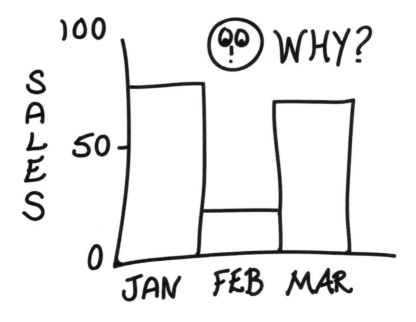

Simple histograms can be presented in sketches

Histograms have bars going up vertically and require the data in a particular sequence (e.g. months of the year along a horizontal axis). Bar charts, on the other hand, may have the blocks either vertically or horizontally aligned and data do not have to be in a particular sequence.

The very simple histogram above shows sales in the first three months of the year. Sketching this on a flipchart would be easy.

Histogram: with lines added

Drawing graphs informally makes it easy to add lines and written comments

This example shows how you can draw the graph first and then add to it. In this instance the arrow can be added afterwards to show the downward trend. Equally, the stick figure drawing and the words 'next steps' could be also added after the initial drawing.

Similarly, one can imagine making notes on or around the graphs as you discuss them with a group.

Colours may be used effectively to draw additional marks to show, for example, the comparison with last year or even to draw projections for the next few months. Therefore, drawing by hand does give you some flexibility because of the opportunity to add to the image whilst discussing it.

Choices for presenting graphs

Everything we talked about in previous chapters regarding presenting will apply to graphs. However, given that you are not showing the image electronically you would want to make a virtue out of presenting it by hand. In other words, it would be desirable if the effect of presenting it by hand is even better than if you had presented it electronically.

As with everything else we have talked about, you will be able to present your hand-drawn graph using different methods.

Pre-prepared

If you are going to show a graph that is completely pre-prepared and you are not going to add anything to it as you speak, this is better shown electronically. This is because you are not actually making a difference with your drawing skills, unless you have chosen to draw it in a way that could not have been done electronically.

Partly prepared

This, in my view, is where you can make a good case for doing a graph by hand. The fact that it is partly prepared means that you have the opportunity to draw certain key parts of the graph accurately in advance. You can then reserve your 'live' drawing input for adding in the content of the graph in dramatic ways.

On-the-fly: 'live'

As discussed before, drawing the whole thing 'live' is a great way to hook attention. I would, however, ensure that the graph really is simple enough to be able to build it up 'live' from scratch. As with other examples of 'live' drawing, this often is the most engaging way to present a graph.

Both electronic and hand-drawn

It is perfectly possible and useful to sketch a hand-drawn graph either before or after showing an electronic version.

This could be for the purpose of discussion where the ability to spontaneously add further lines and notes is easily done on your hand-drawn version. Extra lines could represent 'what-if' scenarios or be useful for looking at trends.

For this purpose the hand-drawn version need not even be exactly to scale or even contain all the detail. In fact, it would almost certainly work better as a simplified version, or at least an approximation of the original. As long as people can see the points you are making, then it will do the job well.

Tips on presenting your graphs

We will now look at ways that you can:

- motivate people to be interested in your data;
- create curiosity;
- get people anticipating what is coming next;
- make the graph really easy to understand;
- make the experience interactive rather than just passive;
- make your key point with impact.

Introduce the graph before you show it

This is especially useful for pre-prepared graphs. People generally take in information best when they get an overview first. They like to get the big picture up front and then be presented with the detail in such a way that they can see how it fits in. Therefore, introducing a graph before you show it can be really beneficial.

There are a number of ways to do this, which also create motivation to listen, curiosity and anticipation and can make the experience two-way. Consider the following introductions to a graph:

> *'I am going to show you a graph of the production costs for each quarter of this year. Take a look at quarter three. I wonder if you are as surprised as I was.'*

In this example, not only am I introducing the graph but I am giving the group something to look for when they see it. This ensures that, as the graph is shown, they pay attention to the area that I want them to. I have also created some intrigue and curiosity by making the experience active.

Here is another example:

> *'I am going to show you a graph of last year's profits for each of the three companies we are looking at buying. I wonder if you can guess which is which?'*

Again, I have given an overview but this time I have posed the question, which means that once the group looks at the graph they are actively seeking to answer it.

The approach I describe above means that rather than it being a passive experience, it becomes a two-way activity. In this way the audience are involved and are mentally engaged in the material.

Make it a story

Your role is to bring the data to life and one great way to do that is to tell it like a story. People find it much easier to listen when you explain things in this way.

When drawing on-the-fly keep them guessing what's coming next

Use all the principles that we discussed earlier in this book to really keep people fully engaged. So whether you are drawing totally 'live' or completing a partly prepared drawing, seek every opportunity to keep people really wondering what is coming next.

I previously mentioned asking questions when drawing 'live' and this technique applies just as much to graphs. The great thing about drawing a graph 'live' is that you have a lot of flexibility and control with the way you interact with the audience as you are building it up. Your ability in the moment to stop or start drawing can make all the difference in creating intrigue and impact.

Risks and problems of presenting graphs 'live'

The main issues relate to the following.

Where the effect is not enhanced by drawing on-the-fly

Remember that the purpose of sketching a graph by hand is to achieve benefits for the audience in terms of the impact of the presentation. In a quick stroke of the pen you can make lines go up and down exactly in synchronisation with your voice. This kind of method can really enhance the dramatic effect of certain graphs.

However, there will be other graphs where the volume and/or nature of the data shown simply does not lend itself to a hand drawing. The fact is that you do want to end up with a graph that is easy to view when you complete it.

If you have a graph that just takes too long to draw this might also be a reason for adopting a different method. On the one hand people can be very engaged when you draw. However, they will not sit happily for ages whilst you attempt to sketch details of a rather complex graph.

Be prepared to have a go

Take even informal opportunities just to have a go. Sometimes the chance presents itself through necessity. In a meeting you may find yourself wanting to explain an idea or some statistics. In the absence of a pre-prepared graph, a quick sketch often will be enough to get the idea across.

Summary

- Decide when a graph is best presented electronically rather than drawn by hand.

- Draw by hand when doing so will have a positive impact.

- Tell the story of your graph to bring it to life.

- Create curiosity and surprise when drawing graphs 'live' or showing pre-prepared versions.

- When drawing 'live' add lines, numbers and labels at the precise moments to create impact.

- Ask questions to actively involve your audience, rather than regarding people as passive recipients.

- Use contrasting colours to draw attention to important points on graphs and charts.

More practice

Have a go at any of these that you find helpful:

- Draw a line graph to illustrate a trend in your field of work.
- Draw a pie chart with pictures to illustrate an aspect of your work.
- Draw a histogram that represents some important information relating to your business.

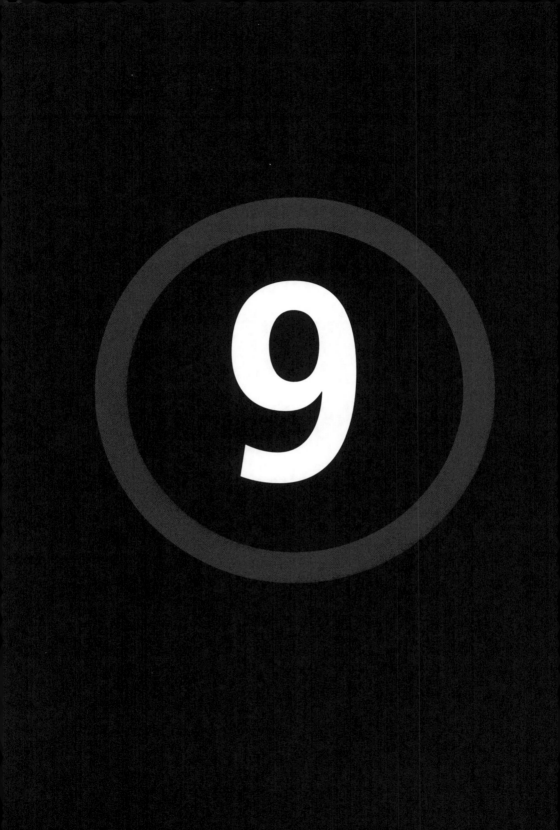

Brilliant bullet points

Why not just words?

You may be wondering why something as straightforward as bullet points needs pictures. Surely the nature of a bullet point is that it is brief and therefore easy to understand and recall. Some people might think that adding pictures is unnecessary elaboration. Whilst all of this sounds reasonable, and words alone are frequently all that is required, the key point is that, in most instances, when we do not use pictures we are missing a trick.

A picture for each bullet point makes it memorable

Creating curiosity and motivation to listen

We can significantly add to levels of engagement, curiosity and interest through the way in which we actually create bullet points as we are speaking. Using pictures gives us much more scope to do this because we can grab attention as people watch a picture develop.

Making it memorable

If we think about the purpose of bullet points, the intention is to convey the essence of what we are saying in the simplest form. The very nature of bullet points is that the detailed information about them is excluded. What could be simpler than that, you might ask? The answer is, in this instance, that we not talking about making it even simpler, we are talking about making it more memorable. Using pictures helps us to do that.

Making it multi-sensory

The use of pictures to accompany bullet points really does give us the opportunity to engage the senses in a more powerful way than just text. As well as the audience *reading* the bullet points they will be *seeing* our pictures and *hearing* our spoken words. Combining the pictures with the words enables us much more easily to trigger *feelings* associated with our bullet points. This enables us to create emotional connections that are not only powerful in themselves, but also assist us in ensuring that our points are memorable.

Tips for Bullet Points

When you have a lot of information – use lower case letters

One of the reasons why lower case letters are easier to read than capitals is because each word has its own unique overall shape. This makes it easier for the eye to distinguish when there are many words on the page. Books are written in lower case, which makes them easy to read. By contrast, when words are written in capitals they all have the overall shape of a rectangle.

See the examples below:

Here you can see two words written in both lower and upper case. I have drawn a line around each word to indicate its overall shape. Each word in lower case has its own distinctive shape. However, the line drawn around each of the words in capitals always forms a rectangle and therefore the overall shape of both words is the same. It is no surprise, therefore, that books and newspapers appear in lower case, thus making large areas of text easy to read. Only headlines tend to be written in capitals.

Capitals work well when you have just a few bullet points

In my experience, using capitals on a flipchart works well providing there is not too much information on the page. Therefore, when creating bullet points for flipcharts, I often use capitals if there are just three or four bullet points.

Use alternating colours

Where you have many lines of text on a flipchart you can alternate colours for each line, thus making each line stand out. For example, alternating black and blue text will be easier to read than a page of all one colour.

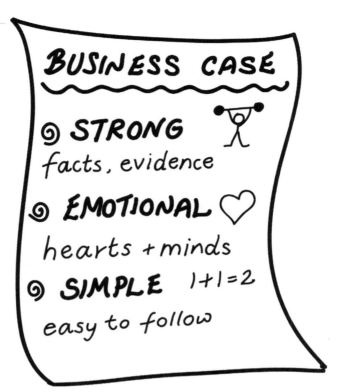

Example using both capitals and lower case writing

This example shows how main headings still stand out when sub-points are in lower case letters. This is a good example of a visual that can be built up 'live' from a blank start. Keeping the pictures this simple means you can easily draw them as you speak. In doing so you keep the group's attention firmly fixed on the visual.

This format also gives you the opportunity to include the group's contributions, e.g. you could come up with the main headings yourself but ask the group for the sub-points.

Using different colours for the bullet points and pictures would create additional visual contrast and therefore make the information stick more easily in the mind.

Using rhythm and repetition

Rhythm can work really well for memory, especially when you have a list of bullet points that are just one word per line.

Let us look at an example where I have used rhythm and repetition. I often tell students that if we *see* something as well as *hear* it, *say* it and *do* it, then we are more likely to remember it.

In order to teach this point I created the bullet point flipchart below which I draw 'live'. By drawing the flipchart and then saying the words; *'see, hear, say, do'* in a rhythm it makes it very easy to remember. Repeating the rhythm a few times makes it even more memorable.

Our brains love rhythm – use it to make ideas stick

Using rhyme

Rhyme is an extremely powerful way of remembering and can be used easily in conjunction with rhythm and pictures. In fact a phrase that rhymes is almost certain to acquire a rhythm when repeated. People naturally will put the emphasis on the same words. Again, this occurs in everyday life, for example *'A stitch in time saves nine.'*

The power of threes

It is amazing how threes work really well in delivering messages. When you have three points to say it is easy to say them with a rhythm and power that creates impact. This effect is seen often in speeches of politicians and other people in the public eye. I recall a political party in the UK saying that the priorities were 'education, education, education'. This shows that it works well even when each bullet point is the same word.

Let us look at a few examples:

- innovation;
- design;
- delivery.

Threes are easy to remember – and fit on flipcharts really well

The power of threes works especially well when they are linked in some way, for example in a time sequence or cause-effect relationship such as the following example:

- listen;
- think;
- respond.

A three-step sequence works well for memorising required actions

Start with the same letter

People find it easy to remember bullet points starting with the same letter. Here are some examples:

- distributing;
- directly;
- daily.

- presence;
- power;
- punch.

Static or active words?

One interesting consideration is whether you choose static or active words. Each has its merits and will feel different as people read or hear them.

Read the following pair of contrasting lists and notice how you feel as you read them:

- innovation;
- communication;
- education.

- innovating;
- communicating;
- educating.

There are merits to both static and active versions but there is no doubt that they feel different. Static words sometimes can come across as rather conceptual. This seems to be the case especially in words that end in '–tion'. The active versions seem to have a momentum about them and, feel more lively and energetic. Typically, verbs ending in 'ing' will create a sense of movement and action.

Make sets of words all active or all static – not mixed

In other words, if you are saying words in threes, they sound better if they are of the same type. Thus, *'listening, learning, growing'* sounds better than *'listening, learning, grow'*.

Find the story – or narrative around your bullet points

Often you will find that you can create a story for your bullet points. This provides a way of creating interest and building up the bullet points in a way that is engaging. We are, therefore, simply adding another memory device by using this method.

If it is not exactly a story, often you will find that a narrative develops around the bullet points. As you explain each one you could elaborate and clarify using examples, evidence or whatever else will help to make your point convincing to the group.

Example formats for bullet points

We have already seen some bullet point designs. Let us now explore example formats further. The following suggestions will give you some choices when creating bullet point lists of your own.

Straight list of bullet points

A straight list is probably the most basic format. Bullet points are simply listed as we have seen in some earlier examples and in the following design:

- global;
- fast;
- delivery.

This example shows that even writing just one word per line and drawing a simple picture for each can convey your idea easily.

It is easy to see that this flipchart could be drawn 'on-the-fly' thus keeping the focus of the group on the visual as you create it.

Bullet list with another word added

I have taken a flipchart shown in an earlier example and added a word vertically. This design can be applied to many situations, in particular those where there is a cause-effect relationship between the bullet points and the other word.

Cause-effect relationship between the bullet list and the word on the right

In this example the point is that, if we learn by *seeing, hearing, saying* and *doing* we actually *remember* information better than if we do not use all of these methods. It is easy for us to link the four words with the one on the right as we build up the visual. This kind of design really enables you to build an interesting story or narrative with the bullet points leading up to a result represented by a key word on the right-hand side.

Bullets but just one picture

In the following example, you will see that there is not a picture for each of the bullet points. Instead I have drawn a picture that represents the overall idea.

The phrase 'thinking correctly under pressure', reduced to 'T-CUP', was used by World Cup winning England rugby coach Sir Clive Woodward.

It so happens that, in this example, a mnemonic ensures that it is easy to recall the concept. The picture is a strong way to further embed the idea in the memory.

One picture makes the whole phrase memorable

How to get the best effect out of your bullet points

It is worth thinking about how you are going to get your bullet points across really effectively. In this regard, as we discussed before, you might decide whether you are going to have them:

- pre-prepared;
- partly prepared; or
- draw them on-the-fly – 'live'.

Any of the above will work and we have discussed the various merits of each option for engaging groups already.

Other points for consideration are as follows:

- **Just present the information, i.e. don't ask the group to contribute.** This keeps you in complete control and means that you know in advance how it will work.
- **Present some bullets and ask the group for additional ideas.** This is an effective option when you want to present a bullet point but then ask the group for some supporting points. You can then write their contributions underneath your main bullet points in the way that we have already seen.
- **Ask the group for bullet points, i.e. just use their contributions.** This is useful when you are happy to receive whatever ideas the group might come up with.

Create your own variations

The examples I have given in this section give good templates for creating more variations of your own. You can create hundreds of different examples using the formats seen in this chapter.

As you get used to using drawing skills to enhance bullet points, begin experimenting and just see what ideas work best.

Don't wait to do everything perfectly

Remember that success in getting your ideas across does not depend on the drawings being perfect. Even a very modest drawing of a symbol or picture will be enough to create a powerful visual association.

Just start and the ideas will flow

When you are thinking up a bullet point flipchart it pays just to start writing or drawing. Do not feel that you have to imagine it all in your head first or get the complete idea before you start drawing. I have found that if I just get started ideas will develop from there. When you get used to adding sketches to bullet points, you will soon find that the ideas come more easily. As you practise more you will find it easier.

Enjoy the positive reactions

By enhancing the words in bullet points with your sketches soon you will start to see the positive reactions from your audience. You will find that they are able to absorb your ideas more easily and your points will be all the more memorable.

The great thing is you can apply your bullet point techniques to numerous topics and get great results time after time.

Summary

- Draw a picture for each bullet point to make it memorable.

- Use colours that match the ideas (e.g. black for negative, yellow for positive).

- Write in capitals where you have just a few lines.

- Write in lower case and alternate colours where you need to write many lines.

- Use rhythm and rhyme to make ideas memorable.

- Tell a story with your bullet points – make them more than just a list.

- Remember to use the power of threes when it makes sense – for increased impact.

- Stick to active or static words in bullet lists – do not mix the two types.

More practice

Have a go at any of the exercises below that are relevant to you, in order to build your skills.

- Take a piece of paper and a pen and sketch a design for the following two sets of bullet points. Just write the words in a list and see what pictures you can come up with to go with each word. Use colours, if available, otherwise just black and white is fine.

  - idea;
  - design;
  - action.

  - individual;
  - team;
  - harmony.

- Think of a topic related to your work. Write down three words in a bullet point list that describe aspects of it. Now draw a picture or symbol to represent each bullet point.

- Look at an existing presentation that has bullet points. Sketch some pictures or symbols that would bring each one to life.

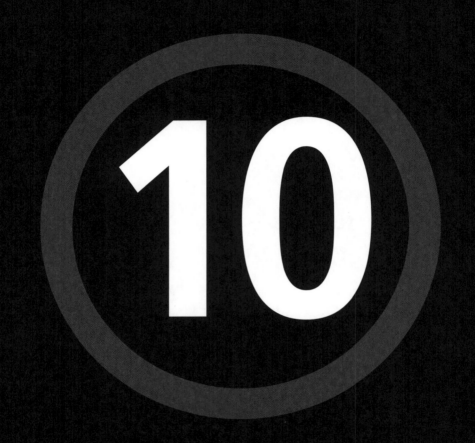

Visual mapping

In this chapter we will look at using our drawings to explain whole topics in ways that are easy to absorb and remember. Specifically, we will look at creating visual maps to bring subjects to life and captivate your audience.

This is an excellent way for teams or individuals to share their ideas in engaging ways. The whiteboards and facilitation boards mentioned earlier are just brilliant for this. However, even a piece of flipchart paper stuck to the wall in landscape orientation will do just fine.

Here is an example of a visual map based on McCarthy's four Ps of marketing.

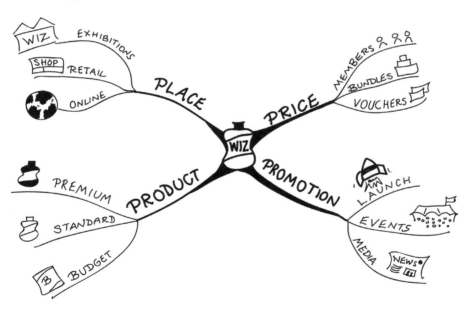

Just by looking at the example you will see that a whole topic is shown by having the main heading in the centre and the various sections branching out. Each branch then has further branches to show the detail. This principle of radiating out from the centre is important when presenting our ideas in a map.

Such visual maps are excellent when we want to explain a whole topic to a group. We need to understand the principles of successful mapping and, just as importantly, how we draw the map 'live' in front of a group.

Why use a map to present a topic?

The potential benefits of using mapping in the field of teaching and learning are well-documented. Colin Rose, a principle exponent of accelerated learning, refers to 'learning maps' in his book *Master and Faster* and says:

> *'Because the information is visual it's possible to take it in all at once and, after a little study, to picture it in your mind's eye.'*

Oliver Caviglioi and Ian Harris refer to 'visible thinking' and use the term 'model maps'. In their book *Mapwise*, they write that such maps are useful for people to be able to externalise their internal thinking:

> *'If their thinking is spread out onto a map, understanding can be both communicated and developed.'*

Let's look in more detail at why a visual map lends itself to presenting topics in ways that groups can easily absorb.

Spatial memory

When you draw, for example on a whiteboard, people have an amazing ability to remember where pictures and symbols are located on different parts of the board.

Even looking at a blank board Spike can still recall the visual map that was there moments ago

I have demonstrated this countless times by drawing a complete map on a whiteboard in front of audiences ranging from business people to students and children. Once I have completed the map, I spin the board around to show a totally blank whiteboard to the group. I ask them to imagine they can still see the complete coloured map.

I then ask them questions about the map and ask them to point to places on the board to indicate various elements I have drawn. Even though the board is blank, they are easily able to point correctly to different parts of the map as they answer my questions. They have no trouble when I ask them questions about the information. The audiences are always amazed at how easily they can answer the questions and point to the correct place. This is all despite the fact that they have made no apparent effort to learn the material.

This has a staggering effect on people's perception of their ability to learn and also their confidence because, typically, they believe that learning requires a lot of effort. Furthermore, most people believe that they are not good at learning and are therefore surprised at the positive results.

Radiant thinking – the map's structure mirrors how the brain works

Tony Buzan, in *The Mind Map Book*, describes the brain's thinking pattern as:

'a gigantic Branching Association Machine (BAM), a super bio-computer with lines of thought radiating from a virtually infinite number of data nodes. This structure reflects the neuronal networks that make up the physical architecture of your brain.'

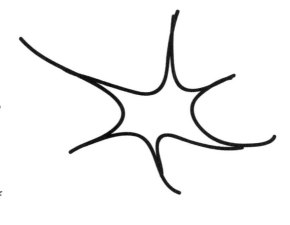

Hence, in mirroring this structure, our maps will always start in the centre and branch outwards with radiating lines. The information is arranged in an ordered way where it is easy to see how one part relates to the other. Therefore, when maps are organised in this way, rather than randomly, they are much easier to remember.

The brain loves to get the big picture first

Most people find it easier to learn if they get the overall idea first and only then focus on the details. It is amazing how much information people can absorb when they receive it in an ordered way rather than in some random fashion. By drawing a map that has the big ideas on the main branches and the detail on the sub-branches it is easy for us to see the big picture and how everything else fits in.

Visual maps show information in memorable chunks

A visual map makes it easier for us remember information by grouping it into chunks, i.e. the main branches are the big chunks.

MEMORABLE CHUNKS

If we think about remembering telephone numbers, we can remember them more easily if we group numbers together.

Many opportunities for us to make ideas memorable

Drawing a map gives us lots of ways to draw, write and say things in ways that stand out.

When we create a map we can include many techniques that help people remember:

- humour in pictures and in what we say;
- striking colours, shapes and lines;
- the unusual, something different or quirky.

One of the great reasons why drawing maps 'live' works so well is that when people see the start of something they are always curious to see how it finishes. This happens when people watch films and television dramas, or read a gripping novel. Once they are hooked, they are really keen to see how the story ends. We can achieve the same effect when we are creating a map to explain a topic.

It can be quick

Using this method is a really fast way of getting a topic across to a group. In fact, in my experience, when drawing and speaking at the same time I find that people can listen very easily to a fast-paced talk.

Drawing the pictures and writing as you talk really keeps people engaged and it is often possible to convey a great deal of information about a topic even within the space of 10 or 15 minutes. From the listeners' point of view they probably do not want to be listening for much longer anyway. If you needed a lot longer to explain something it would probably be helpful to do something to break it up. You could, for example, explain part of it with a different method, or change the pace by giving time to reflect or ask questions before moving onto another section.

The drawings do not even have to be especially neat and tidy, which is great news. Once you start sketching, people will remember even quickly drawn rough sketches just as well as those that are perfectly drawn. It is often better to keep the pace up than dwell on drawing everything perfectly.

Those watching can be relaxed yet alert

The beauty of presenting a topic in this way is how people feel while you are speaking. This style of presenting naturally induces a state of relaxed alertness which is highly conducive to the absorption of information with apparent lack of effort.

This is very different from other states that the audience may often be experiencing. As an example, sometimes when people are really bored their level of alertness drops and they approach what might be described as a sleepy or drowsy state.

It is clear, therefore, that there are numerous reasons why it makes sense to consider visual mapping as a way of presenting entire topics. Let us take a look now at what kinds of topics may be suitable for this method.

What kinds of topics might we present using a map?

Almost any topic is capable of being translated into a map:

- features and benefits of a new product;
- a problem in the business;
- creative business ideas;
- a solution;
- a business plan;
- a strategy;
- how the organisation works.

However, the key thing for us to consider is which kinds of topics not only lend themselves to visual mapping, but are also suitable to be presented by drawing as we speak.

Topics with a few sections are ideal for presenting 'live'

When drawing 'live' use visual mapping for topics that ideally have up to five sections, or a maximum of about seven. Any more than that means it is likely that the map will take you too long to draw and this can have an adverse impact on your audience's attention.

Pre-prepared maps could have more sections

Pre-prepared maps are quicker to explain and therefore may contain more branches without adversely affecting audience engagement.

The pre-prepared versions do work really well when teams are creating maps, for example to show their ideas. Working in small groups, teams can create their maps to reflect their discussions as they go along. They can then present their completed maps to colleagues.

How to draw a visual map

It is essential to plan a map first if you are to get the best result. Even just a rough sketch will ensure that you have all the elements set out properly.

Visual map design

There are a few rules to follow to ensure you do create your map properly – otherwise it might not be so memorable. The first thing we need to look at is the design of the map itself. The following steps will show you how to create the basic structure and then there are tips on how to enhance its effectiveness.

Here are the steps to building your map:

1 Have your paper in landscape orientation – it is easier than portrait orientation to set out your ideas and for people to take them in.
2 Start in the centre – draw a picture or symbol to represent the topic and write a topic name.
3 Draw branches for the main ideas – for each chunk of the topic draw a line outwards.
4 Label each of these main branches ideally with one word – or a brief heading.
5 Draw sub-branches off each branch – and label these along the lines with capitals.

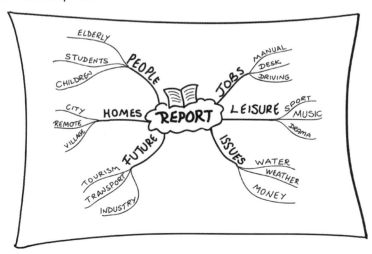

6 Now add pictures or symbols to go with your words, and place pictures near the corresponding words.

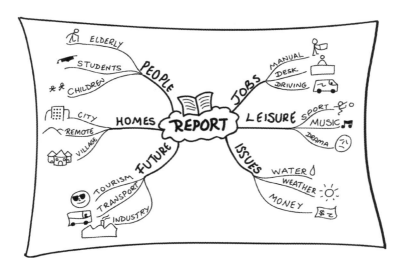

7 Check the whole map – this is a chance to check that all the information is arranged in a way that makes sense hierarchically. For example, check if you have come up with any subheading branches that should really be elevated to the status of main ideas or vice versa.

8 Redraw your map to make it even better and, most importantly, memorable – inevitably, in the initial drafting a map's elements will not necessarily appear exactly as you might want them in a finished version. Therefore, this is a chance to refine the design and check that everything is in order.

Tips to enhance its effectiveness

- **Arrange branches evenly around the page.** This will give it a sense of order compared with drawing them in a more random way. It will be more appealing to the eye.

- **Use colours.** You may use colour coding for repeated ideas and this will make it much easier for people to focus on key ideas.

- **Print clearly.** Capital letters typically work best.

- **Use one word for labels.** Wherever possible reduce labels to just one word. If you cannot keep a label to one word, at least make it as short as possible.
- **Make sure every word or phrase is accompanied by a picture or symbol.** In this way you are creating a link between the word and picture. By binding them together they will be so much easier to remember.
- **Write words near to the corresponding pictures.** When a word is right next to a picture we connect the two much more easily than if it is somewhat separate. Therefore, make sure you write a label very close to the picture it describes. Likewise, when labelling a branch, make the word go along the branch.
- **Write bigger for the main ideas.** People are used to the idea of more important things being bigger (e.g. chapter headings in books are bigger than sub-headings).
- **Keep the pictures simple.** This will help to make it easy to draw them 'live' in front of a group.
- **Write words in a way that reinforces the idea where appropriate.** For example, if 'tall' is written in tall letters or 'debt' is written in red, it will be easier to recall. I would not recommend doing this all the time but using this technique where appropriate does make words stand out.
- **Ensure that you have plenty of white space.** If the drawing is too crowded it makes it more difficult to see the information clearly. Plenty of white space makes it more appealing to the viewer and visually calmer.

Have a go

Pick a topic that you might speak about, something you know well. This could be a business topic, a hobby or interest.

Sketch a map to show the topic, including pictures as well as words.

Presenting a visual map

Do keep in mind all the principles mentioned earlier about presenting, especially if you are drawing 'live' to explain your map. If you follow those ideas, this will help you to deliver your talk successfully.

Here is a great additional tip that works well when using visual mapping in training:

Ask them to recreate the map – let them surprise themselves.

It may not be appropriate to test people's memory in a presentation or a meeting, but, if you use this technique in a training situation, it is a valid activity and really helpful. It is very easy to test people on how well they have remembered the information presented on one of these maps.

How to check memory and reinforce learning

First, complete the map without interruption. Then remove the map from their sight. If you have drawn the map on flipchart paper, you could remove it to reveal a blank sheet of paper behind it.

Then I will ask people to work in pairs using A4 paper and coloured pens to recreate what they have just seen. If you want to make it slightly easier you could always draw the main branches on the blank paper. In this way they can see the framework but still have to recall all the words and pictures. They always remember most, if not all, of the map and often are surprised at just how much they can recall. Their success creates a positive atmosphere, and also reinforces their learning, which is a good confidence booster.

Benefits of communicating with visual maps

It works

You will actually find that people will be able to grasp your entire topic and its details very easily. It is therefore a very effective way to get a lot of information across to a group.

It's different from what may be expected

Creating a map will engage people in a different way than they are typically used to in a business presentation. People are used to seeing electronic presentations, so this will definitely be something out of the ordinary for most people. This difference typically will be perceived as something creative and unusual and the fact that the information will be memorable will demonstrate the value of this approach.

It's informal and doesn't need special equipment

Other than some coloured flipchart pens and paper no other equipment is needed. If a whiteboard is not available, paper simply can be fixed to the wall.

It's impressive and enjoyable

People are always very impressed and find it an enjoyable way to learn.

So enjoy creating some topic maps for your own content and trying out the technique. Remember, it still works if the drawings are not perfect, so just have a go!

Summary

- Use maps for information or topics with around five–seven sections.
- Draw branches and sub-branches that are evenly spaced.

- Write one-word labels wherever possible.

- Use varying colours and, where possible, match the colour to the idea.

- Use emphasis in your voice to make elements memorable.

- Decide the best place to start when drawing 'live'.

- Ask a group to recreate a map if you want to see if they can remember it (e.g. in training).

More practice

Select any of the following exercises that are most relevant and helpful to you.

- Choose a topic you need to explain to a group and create a visual map to explain it.

- Choose a non-work topic you know well and create a map to illustrate it.

- Choose a topic relevant to your business (e.g. how your organisation works). Draw a map to illustrate it.

Your visual toolkit

I have devised this for you to look through in case you want some inspiration. You may like to use some of these or they may spark further ideas. I have covered a lot of the common business themes.

Remember each picture can have many other meanings – they can be used time and time again!

Actions

Agreement

Collaboration

Communication

Data

Direction

Energy

Expressions

Goal

Global

Ideas

Innovation

Journey

 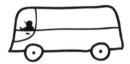 

Knowledge

Leadership

Manufacturing

Obstacles

People at work

Performance

Profit

Research

Retail

Strategy

Time

Index

Do you want your people to be the very best at what they do?

Talk to us about how we can help.

As the world's leading learning company, we know a lot about what your people need in order to be better at what they do.

Whatever subject or skills you've got in mind (from presenting or persuasion to coaching or communication skills), and at whatever level (from new-starters through to top executives) we can help you deliver tried-and-tested, essential learning straight to your workforce – whatever they need, whenever they need it and wherever they are.

Talk to us today about how we can:

- Complement and support your existing learning and development programmes
- Enhance and augment your people's learning experience
- Match your needs to the best of our content
- Customise, brand and change it to make a better fit
- Deliver cost-effective, great value learning content that's proven to work.

Contact us today:
corporate.enquiries@pearson.com